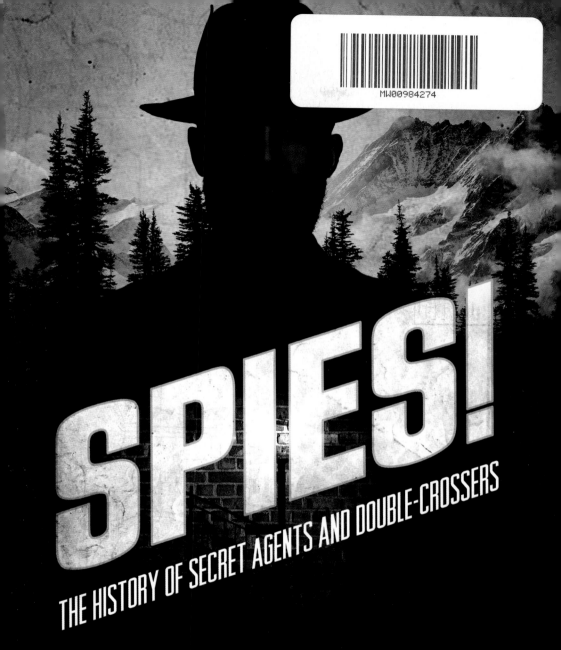

SPIES!

THE HISTORY OF SECRET AGENTS AND DOUBLE-CROSSERS

BY REBECCA LANGSTON-GEORGE
AND ALLISON LASSIEUR

Capstone Young Readers
a capstone imprint

Spies! The History of Secret Agents and Double-Crossers is published by
Capstone Young Readers
1710 Roe Crest Drive
North Mankato, Minnesota 56003

www.mycapstone.com

Library of Congress Cataloging-in-Publication Data is available on the Library of Congress website.

ISBN 978-1-62370-911-2 (paperback)

ISBN 978-1-62370-920-4 (eBook)

Summary: Immerse yourself in the dangerous and daring lives of real-life spies. Using vivid images
supplemented with maps and timelines, you can live the experience of some of the most notorious and
ingenious spies in four different eras. Traveling through the 20th century and beyond, you'll learn about
the different ways spies have navigated through the world.

Content Consultant: Joseph Fitsanakis, PhD,
Intelligence and National Security Studies Program, Coastal Carolina University

Designer: Russell Griesmer

For photo credits, see the endmatter

Printed and bound in China

TABLE OF CONTENTS

CYBER SPIES AND SECRET AGENTS OF MODERN TIMES

SPIES!

COURAGEOUS SPIES AND INTERNATIONAL INTRIGUE OF WORLD WAR I

World War I started with a literal bang—the assassination of the Austro-Hungarian monarch, Franz Ferdinand. But the tensions that led up to the declaration of war had been brewing for decades.

In 1908, Austria-Hungary, worried that its hold in the Slavic region was waning, took over the twin provinces of Bosnia-Herzogovina. Serbia was furious because it considered Bosnia to be part of the Serbian homeland. So Serbian and Bosnian nationalists began a campaign to gain back their homeland.

Meanwhile, France and Russia, angry about Germany taking land from earlier wars, entered into an alliance. Great Britain became a part of this alliance because it was worried about Germany's growing navy. These three powers—France, Russia, and Great Britain—became known as the Triple Entente.

Germany had supported Austria-Hungary for years. So when Austria-Hungary's monarch, the Archduke Franz Ferdinand, was assassinated by a Bosnian nationalist, Germany pledged its support to Austria-Hungary. With that support, Austria-Hungary declared war on Serbia in 1914 and what was then known as the Great War began.

The war spanned most of the globe. The Allies included Great Britain, France, Belgium, Italy (which first sided with the Central Powers), Japan, Serbia, and later in the war, the United States. The Central Powers were Germany, Austria-Hungary, the Ottoman Empire, and Bulgaria. The empires with colonies enlisted the countries they ruled into the fight, bringing in India, South Africa, Brazil, Canada, and many others.

After four long years of battle, the Central Powers began to surrender one by one. Finally, Germany surrendered on November 11, 1918, signing an armistice, or ceasefire. The number of soldiers who died in the war has been estimated at about 10 million. The number of civilians who died is estimated to be between 6 million and 10 million. The war was named "the war to end all wars," but as history teaches, this was not to be. This section tells the stories of a few courageous spies and the international intrigue they navigated during a war that was unlike any other in history.

Gavrilo Princip joined the Black Hand society and became

CHAPTER 1

GAVRILO PRINCIP: THE BLACK HAND AND THE START OF THE WAR

Gavrilo Princip (ga-VRIL-low PRIN-sip) had to kill himself. He pushed through the crowds that had come to see the heir to the throne of Austria-Hungary, Archduke Franz Ferdinand, drive through the streets of Sarajevo, Bosnia, on June 28, 1914. The archduke and his wife, Sophie, were in the city to dedicate a new hospital. Gavrilo's orders had been simple: assassinate the archduke and then commit suicide. He had failed at the first thing. He couldn't fail at the second.

Gavrilo was a member of the secret Black Hand society, a group dedicated to the unification of the Serbian people. He and six other spy-terrorists had been ordered to the streets of Sarajevo that morning, all with the goal of killing the archduke.

PLANNING THE ASSASSINATION

That spring the head of the Black Hand, Colonel Dragutin Dimitrijević (Dra-GOO-tin Dim-EE-tree-Yay-vich), known as

Franz Ferdinand was the archduke
of Austria-Hungary.

Apis, decided it was time to do something big. The archduke was the future ruler of Austria-Hungary. What better way to fight the hated occupier than to kill its leader? Apis recruited a group of teenagers into the Black Hand, including Gavrilo.

As a member of the Black Hand society, Gavrilo and the others swore to assassinate the archduke. The Black Hand leaders gave these new recruits guns and grenades, and helped get them to Sarajevo. Then each recruit got something even more deadly: a pill filled with the poison cyanide and orders to commit suicide when the mission was done.

On that sunny morning, the seven recruits took up positions along the archduke's route. If the first person failed, the job fell to the next, and so on down the line. The archduke's motorcade of six cars left the train station mid-morning and headed to the outskirts of town. This was the moment the Black Hand assassins had been waiting for.

DID YOU KNOW?

The members of the Black Hand worked
together in cells of three to five.
Black Hands didn't know anyone outside
their cells. Each cell got its orders
from a high-ranking leader.

The first Black Hand recruit in line, Mohamed Mehmedbašić (mo-HAH-med MEH-met-BAYSH-itch), didn't throw his grenade because a police officer was standing nearby. Down the road, next in line, Nedeljko Čabrinović (neh-DEL-ko ca-BRIN-o-vich) threw his grenade—but it bounced off the archduke's car and exploded under a car behind. Čabrinović swallowed his cyanide pill and jumped into the Miljacka River, hoping to die. But the pill only made him vomit and the river was just a few inches deep, so he didn't drown. Instead, he was quickly arrested.

The archduke's motorcade sped past the other Black Hand assassins one by one. None used their weapons as the cars passed. The crowds were too thick, or there wasn't a clear shot. When the motorcade got to Gavrilo's position, the archduke's car was going too fast for him to get a good aim. Gavrilo was afraid he might accidently shoot an innocent bystander in the tightly packed crowds.

As the motorcade sped away, Gavrilo's heart sank. His gun weighed down the pocket of his coat, and he considered using it on himself. He also had the cyanide. Before he killed himself, he went to a sidewalk café on a side street and slumped over a table.

A "LUCKY" BREAK

As he was working up the courage to kill himself, the crowds got louder. Gavrilo looked up and saw a stunning sight. The archduke's car had taken a wrong turn into the narrow side street. It had stopped, fenced in by the crowds. Sitting in the car was the archduke, not five feet in front of him!

Gavrilo couldn't believe his luck. Slowly he stood up and pulled the heavy gun from his pocket. He fired twice. The first bullet hit the archduke's wife, Sophie, in the abdomen. The second shot hit the archduke in the neck. Screams tore through the crowd. A group of men grabbed Gavrilo and threw him to the ground. He didn't care. The archduke and his wife were dead. He had completed the Black Hand's mission.

The archduke and his wife, Sophie, were assassinated in their car.

THE END OF THE BLACK HAND

Gavrilo and Čabrinović were arrested on the spot. While they were in custody they told police the names of the rest of the Black Hand assassins, and they were soon arrested as well. The only one that got away was Mehmedbašić, who escaped and went into hiding. All the remaining assassins were put on trial. The sentence

EYEWITNESS TO AN ASSASSINATION

Count Franz von Harrach, acting as a bodyguard, was in the car with the archduke and his wife. He wrote down what happened after Gavrilo fired his two shots.

As the car quickly reversed, a thin stream of blood spurted from His Highness's mouth on to my right che[e]k. As I was pulling out my handkerchief to wipe the blood away from his mouth, the Duchess cried out to him, "For God's sake! What has happened to you?" At that she slid off the seat and lay on the floor of the car with her face between his knees. I had no idea that she too was hit and thought she had simply fainted with fright. Then I heard His Imperial Highness say, '"Sophie, Sophie, don't die. Stay alive for the children!"

At that, I seized the Archduke by the collar of his uniform, to stop his head dropping forward, and asked him if he was in great pain. He answered me quite distinctly, "It is nothing!" His face began to twist somewhat but he went on repeating, six or seven times, ever more faintly as he gradually lost consciousness, "It's nothing!" Then came a brief pause followed by a convulsive rattle in his throat, caused by loss of blood. This ceased on arrival at the governor's residence.

for murder was death, but these Black Hand spies got lucky. All but one of them were still teenagers. Under the law, because of their age, they could not be executed. Instead, they were all thrown in prison. Gavrilo died of tuberculosis in prison two years later. Others served their time and were released. Only one of the spies, Danilo Ilic, wasn't so lucky. Because he was over 20, he got the death penalty and was executed.

In 1917 the Black Hand was outlawed and Apis and other Black Hand leaders were arrested and executed by Austria-Hungary. But wartime spying was just beginning. Both sides quickly built up their own spy rings. Intelligence gathering and espionage grew into a powerful part of the Great War.

Supporters of Gavrilo Princip attended his trial.

Blinker Hall gathered many different types of
spies for Room 40.

CHAPTER 2

CODE BREAKERS: BLINKER HALL AND THE SPIES OF ROOM 40

It was an ordinary-looking door, just like all the other doors in the British Admiralty building in London, England. The number "40" appeared on the door, along with a small No Admittance sign. What was behind that door? One of the biggest spy secrets of World War I.

The spies who worked in Room 40 didn't carry guns or go on exciting adventures. Their work was more deadly than that. Their job was to decode secret messages sent by the Germans. They had to discover everything the enemy was planning to do. Every secret message they cracked meant dozens, if not hundreds, of people might be saved.

The boss of Room 40 didn't look much like a spy. Sir William Hall was a naval officer with a facial tic that made him blink all the time. Because of it, he got the nickname "Blinker," and it stuck. When the war began, Blinker and other British officers knew they'd need a team of code-crackers in order to win the war. Blinker was the head of British Naval Intelligence, which made him the perfect person to be in charge of a team of spy code breakers.

Blinker Hall's code breakers weren't scientists or math experts. Blinker knew that the best code breakers would be talented in a wide range of skills, from history and languages to cyphers and puzzles. Room 40 spies also needed to be fluent in German.

Room 40 spies came from many different backgrounds. There was Frank Adcock, a college professor who specialized in ancient history. Francis Birch was a brilliant historian and a comic actor. Walter Bruford taught German literature. Alastair Dennison was an Olympic athlete who was fluent in German. Frank Cyril Tiarks was a banker and a member of the British nobility. Dilly Knox studied Greek classics. John Beazley was an expert on ancient Greek vases. Nigel de Grey had been a publisher before he came to Room 40. The Reverend William Montgomery enjoyed translating German religious texts.

"Room 40" was actually composed of three cramped rooms. One of the rooms was a small bedroom with a mouse-infested bed. Throughout the war more code-breaking spies joined the team, and by the end of the war more than 100 code breakers worked in Room 40. At first they took turns working in the small rooms. Later the spies got better offices in the Admiralty Building, but they still called their new space Room 40.

Having brilliant German-speaking code breakers was the first step. Now they had to figure out the German war codes.

(CODE) BOOKS TO DIE FOR

The spies in Room 40 had a secret weapon: not one, but three stolen German codebooks! The Allies got the first codebook when sailors from an Australian ship boarded a German merchant ship off the coast of Melbourne, Australia. The British got the second codebook from the Russians, who'd destroyed a German ship in the Gulf of Finland. Sailors from a British fishing boat pulled a lead-lined chest out of the wreckage of a German ship, and inside was the third codebook. All three codebooks made it to Room 40 in the first few months of the war.

The Germans didn't know their precious codebooks had fallen into enemy hands. The spies in Room 40 started using the codebooks as soon as they got them, deciphering hundreds of messages. But using the German codebooks proved to be trickier, and more dangerous, than the Room 40 spies expected. The Allies knew that if they used all the information from the decoded messages, the Germans would quickly realize that their codes had been broken. So Allied forces had to carefully choose which intelligence they used. Sometimes they had to let German attacks happen, sacrificing Allied lives so their code-breaking secrets would be safe.

The Germans eventually changed some of their codes, but that didn't keep the Room 40 spies from breaking them too. The Germans often sent messages in both the old and new codes, so that their armies would be sure to understand them. That was great for the Room 40 spies. They were able to compare the new codes with the old ones to break the messages. Through most of the war they were able to use the codebooks to read thousands of German messages. They even kept track of German armies and naval fleets. This was especially helpful for the Allied forces. When the war started, the Allies spent a lot of time searching the oceans for enemy ships and submarines. They were afraid of surprise attacks. The Room 40 spies could tell them exactly where all the German forces would be. The Allies didn't have to worry about surprise attacks anymore. They could focus their time and energy on fighting.

THE ZIMMERMAN TELEGRAM

The war dragged on for two and a half terrible years. By 1917 millions of soldiers on both sides were wounded or dead. Neither side was winning. Britain had begged the United States to join the war on their side, but President Woodrow Wilson would not do it. Only something really big could convince him to throw the United States into the war.

On January 17, 1917, two Room 40 spies, the Reverend Montgomery and Nigel de Grey, intercepted a coded German message. It used a code they didn't know, but it was similar to other codes they already knew. Slowly they decoded it, one section at a time. The message had been written by the German foreign minister Arthur Zimmerman, and sent to his German ambassador in Mexico, Heinrich von Eckhardt. As Montgomery and de Grey broke each section of the message, they got more excited. This was bigger than

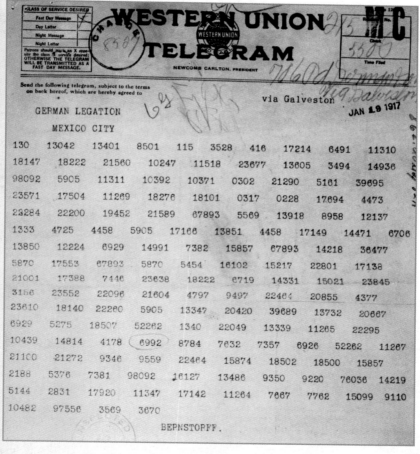

The Zimmerman telegram helped change the course of the war.

anything they'd ever decoded. It was so huge that they didn't even bother cracking the whole message. Instead, they ran to Blinker Hall.

De Grey blurted out, "Do you want America in the war, sir?"

"Yes, why?" Blinker replied.

"I've got a telegram that will bring them in if you give it to them," de Grey replied breathlessly.

Blinker read the half-decoded telegram in shock. The German foreign minister revealed that Germany was going to begin unrestricted submarine warfare. That meant German submarines would attack every ship they saw, including American ships. But the ambassador was worried that this might push the United States to enter the war against Germany. So he made Mexico an unbelievable offer. Germany asked Mexico to start a war with the United States, with Germany's help! If Mexico agreed, Germany would make sure that Mexico would get Texas, New Mexico, and Arizona back from the United States.

A few weeks later the Zimmerman telegram and its explosive message got to President Wilson. He was outraged. But he had promised the people of the United States they would not go to war. He gave the telegram to the newspapers, which splashed it all over their front pages. As predicted, people of the United States were horrified. When President Wilson finally called for war, the country was ready to listen. On April 6, 1917, the United States declared war on Germany and entered World War I.

FATE OF ROOM 40

Cracking the Zimmerman telegram was one of the greatest moments in wartime code breaking. The spies in Room 40 continued to work until the war ended in 1918. After that, most of them went back to the lives they had before the war. But peace didn't last long. In 1939 World War II began in Europe, and many of the Room 40 spies went back to work as code breakers in another world war.

SPY IN THE BATHTUB

Dilly Knox was one of Room 40's top code-breaking spies. He always said he did his best work in the bathtub. Finally, Blinker gave Knox his own office and had a bathtub installed in it just for Knox. Knox liked to work through the night, soaking in the tub and decoding messages.

CHAPTER 3

EDITH CAVELL: THE NURSE WHO SPIED

One early summer day in 1915, nurse Edith Cavell and several other nurses were tending the sick and injured in their Red Cross hospital in Brussels, Belgium. Suddenly, shadows darkened the hallway. The German secret police had come looking for Edith. She was a spy, they said. She was a traitor. They searched but found nothing of value and left. Edith had been warned. The Germans were watching.

What did the German army want with a 49-year-old British nurse? Edith Cavell was part of an underground resistance group that helped more than 200 English soldiers escape the German army during World War I.

NURSE TURNED SPY

Edith never expected to become a spy. She grew up in the English countryside and trained as a nurse in Britain. When she was in her 40s, a friend, Dr. Antoine Depage, asked her to travel to sels, Belgium, to nurse one of his child patients. He saw her

and dedication and asked her to run Belgium's first nurses'

ing school, the Berkendael Medical Institute.   By the time

broke out in 1914, the Berkendael, under Edith's leadership,

among the best in Belgium.

 When the war began, the nursing school was turned into

d Cross hospital, which had a duty to care for all soldiers

rdless of where they were from. Edith's hospital became

vn as a place where everyone would be treated fairly.

When the German army invaded Belgium, the Belgian

rnment abandoned the country. Germany was now in

ith Cavell (bottom row, first on the left) ran a nursing

control of Belgium, and it made some alarming changes. They still allowed Cavell's Red Cross hospital to help everyone, but they ordered that Allied soldiers who had recovered from their injuries had to report to the police. Cavell began to notice that these soldiers were never heard from again. Then on November 1, 1914, two wounded English soldiers, Colonel Dudley Boger and Sergeant Frederick Meachin, appeared at the hospital.

Edith remembered the posters all over Brussels that screamed, "Any Male or Female who hides an English or French soldier in his house shall be severely punished." Edith knew that "punishment" was death by shooting. But she couldn't hand English soldiers over to the Germans. She brought them into the hospital and took care of their wounds. Eventually the soldiers escaped.

Edith used the hospital as a safe house. She would often keep soldiers in the hospital for longer than they needed to be there, to keep them out of German hands for as long as possible. As long as the soldiers were "patients," the Germans left them alone. If the beds were full, Edith put the soldiers in the hospital's attic or cellar. In one year Edith's network saved more than 200 soldiers from the German army.

SECRET MESSAGES

Edith's network also smuggled secret messages to the Allied forces in Britain. Even though Edith and her fellow resisters didn't focus on intelligence, they watched and listened and sent any useful information to the Allies. The soldiers they helped carried these messages—such as the locations of secret German stockpiles of ammunition and gasoline—hidden in the soles of their shoes or in their boots. Sometimes they would write the messages about the locations of German forces and aircraft on handkerchiefs, then sew them into the lining of their clothing.

EDITH'S COVER IS BLOWN

German officers gradually learned about the safe house network Edith worked with. They began secret surveillance of Edith and the nurses who worked with her. Finally the German secret police decided to act.

By then Edith and her fellow spies knew that the Germans were suspicious of them. On that day in 1915 when the German secret police arrived at the hospital, Edith was sure she would be arrested. But one of her nurses, Elizabeth Wilkins, also a spy, saw the soldiers heading to the hospital and immediately realized what was happening. She rushed to Edith's house and hid all the dangerous documents minutes before the Germans arrived. The Germans never found them.

The German secret police detained Wilkins and interrogated her for four hours. She denied any knowledge of a network helping soldiers. Finally the Germans let her go. But they were

DID YOU KNOW?

The International Committee of the
Red Cross (ICRC) was founded in
Switzerland in 1863. Its only purpose,
then and today, is to care for the
victims of wars and armed conflicts
around the world.

on to her and the rest of the spies, and Edith knew it. Edith destroyed all the documents and evidence she had, but she refused to stop spying.

Her friends begged her to leave the country, but she stayed. On July 31, 1915, the German secret police arrested two members of her network. They also confiscated a stack of documents that included the names and addresses of network members. Five days later, Edith and Wilkins were arrested as well. Over the next few weeks, 35 members of Edith's underground network were arrested.

INTERROGATION, TRIAL, AND EXECUTION

Edith sat in a dimly lit room, facing her German interrogator. She admitted to helping more than 200 soldiers escape occupied Belgium. "Had I not helped," she said, "they would have been shot."

Edith's trial only lasted two days. She was sentenced to death, along with others in her organization. But no one really thought the Germans would go through with the execution. Edith admitted only to helping soldiers, not to sending messages. The fact that she'd nursed German soldiers along with Allied troops was in her favor too. But the Germans decided to make an example of Edith. They argued that because of her, Allied soldiers lived to fight against the Germans. Alarmed, diplomats from the

United States and Spain stepped in to defend Edith. The Germans ignored their pleas.

Early on the morning of October 12, 1915, Edith was executed by firing squad and unceremoniously buried at the site.

Her death led to widespread outrage, especially in the United States and Britain.

Edith Cavell was given a death sentence for spying.

Thousands of British men enlisted after her death. Books, songs, and stories of Edith's bravery and honor swept through Britain and the United States. People saw her as a martyr to the Allied cause. Edith Cavell's execution created a wave of anti-German feeling in the United States, and was one of the reasons the United States finally entered World War I eighteen months later. When the war was over, her body was returned to England. Crowds lined the streets as the procession bearing her coffin rolled slowly past.

Sidney Reilly was known as a master of disguises.

CHAPTER 4

SIDNEY REILLY: THE ACE OF SPIES

In August 1918, Sidney Reilly, the "Ace of Spies," got some terrible news. Someone had tried to assassinate Vladimir Lenin, the Bolshevik leader of Russia. That wasn't what worried Sidney. The bad news was that he hadn't been a part of it.

Sidney, along with a small, secret group of spies, had been plotting to overthrow Lenin for weeks. If their mission was a success, the Allies would be closer to winning the Great War. If they failed, they would all be executed. The spy group didn't know the person who had attempted the assassination. What Sidney did know was that now his small group had to move fast. As soon as the Cheka, the Russian secret police, started investigating the assassination, Sidney was sure they'd find out about his spies. Their cover would be blown, and their lives lost—for good.

MYSTERIOUS BEGINNINGS OF A MASTER SPY

Sidney Reilly had faced death many times. Or had he? Sidney would go on to have many nicknames including, "Ace of Spies" and "The Greatest Spy in History." But no one knew his real name. Sometimes he claimed his father was an Irish sea captain, an Irish minister, a Russian aristocrat, or a wealthy landowner from Russia. The most likely story—though never verified—is he was born in Odessa, Ukraine, the son of Russian Jewish parents, and his real name was Sigmund Rosenblum.

The stories Sidney told about his early years were so outlandish that most historians today think he made them all up. According to Sidney, he faked his own death to escape Odessa and stowed away on a ship to South America. Then, he somehow became part of an expedition to the Amazonian jungle. As if that weren't dangerous enough, he bragged that he single-handedly rescued a group of British officers from a tribe of jungle cannibals. Amazingly, one of the officers just happened to be a member of the British Secret Intelligence Service, known as MI1(c) at the time. The officer was so grateful to Sidney for saving his life from the cannibals that he gave the young man money, a British passport, and a job as a spy.

Were these stories true, or cover for a top spy looking to hide his tracks? No one knows. Almost the only thing that can be proven is that Sidney did arrive in London in 1895. By that time he knew several languages, including Russian, German, and English. One fact that everyone agrees on is that in 1909, Sidney was hired, unofficially, of course, to spy for the new Secret Intelligence Bureau.

UNDERCOVER AROUND THE WORLD

In the years before World War I, Sidney traveled the world as one of Britain's most covert spies. By all accounts he was elegant, sophisticated, and charming—perfect qualities for a spy. Sidney had eleven passports with eleven different identities. He had a reputation for ruthlessness: an agent who would poison, stab, shoot, or choke anyone in his way.

One of Sidney's most dangerous missions began in 1909. He had to go undercover and steal plans for German weapons. If he were caught, he would be executed. The story is that Sidney went undercover as a German worker at the Krupps weapons manufacturing plant and generously volunteered to work the night shift. Then he broke into the company's secret files and stole plans for the weapons.

When World War I began, Sidney had been spying for Britain for years. But he, along with the other British agents, had worked in the shadows. The British government hid the agents' existence because they didn't want other world powers to know they had a spy organization. That changed in 1918, when the British government officially acknowledged the British Secret Service.

Finally, Sidney was an "official" secret agent, working with the open support of the government. He got a code name, "Agent ST1." Even though the war was almost over, Sidney was about to start the most dangerous mission of his life.

MISSION: DISASTER

In 1917 World War I raged on in Europe. In Russia, the people revolted against the government. The Bolshevik party and its leader, Vladimir Lenin, overthrew the tsarist government in a series of attacks known as the Russian Revolution. Lenin and the Bolsheviks took power in November 1917. One of the promises Lenin made was to withdraw Russia from the war. Britain and the other Allies went into a panic. They feared that if the Russian forces went home, German armies could easily defeat the Allies and win the war.

Many sources disagree on what came next. According to some sources, the British began plotting to overthrow Lenin and put a new leader in his place. The new leader, they hoped, would keep Russian forces fighting alongside the Allies. Eliminating Lenin was a job for the best spy they had for such a task: Sidney Reilly.

Sidney jumped at the chance to do the mission and was soon in Russia. He made contact with Robert Lockhart, a diplomat and the secret leader of the British spy network there. For weeks in the spring and summer of 1918 a small group of top

DID YOU KNOW?

Sidney Reilly and his World War I adventures
are said to be one of the inspirations for
author Ian Fleming's most famous fictional
spy, James Bond.

spies met in secret and plotted the biggest mission they had ever been given. With the help of their anti-Bolshevik Russian friends, Sidney and the spies would take down Lenin and the entire leadership of the Bolsheviks.

The spies had a bold plan. The Bolshevik leaders were planning a big meeting. First, the spies would make sure all the soldiers assigned to guard Lenin during this meeting were traitors who wanted to overthrow the Bolsheviks. They would bribe the soldiers and other anti-Bolsheviks to attend the meeting. Once all the leaders were inside the meeting room, the guards would shoot Lenin and the other leaders. Sidney and the other spies would be hiding behind curtains with grenades. If something went wrong, they were to use them on the assembled leaders.

They put the plan in place, but almost immediately, things started going wrong. The big Bolshevik meeting was postponed at the last minute, ruining their careful plan. Unknown to them, someone betrayed their group to the Cheka, the Bolshevik police. The Cheka were almost ready to arrest the spies when, on August 30, 1918, a Russian woman named Fanya Kaplan shot and wounded Lenin during one of his speeches. She insisted she acted alone, but the Cheka became nervous. It was time to arrest the British spies.

The British government has denied any involvement in an assassination attempt against Lenin. Some sources say the plot was hatched by a group of Latvian nationalists opposed to Lenin and the Bolshevik movement—that neither Sidney nor Lockhart plotted to kill Lenin. These sources say that the Latvian nationalists set up the British (and were in turn set up by the Cheka). Whatever the story, Sidney escaped only 30 minutes before the Cheka arrived to arrest the British spies. One version of his escape story says he paid 60,000 rubles to a smuggler to get him out of Russia. He finally made it back to London. The Bolshevik government sentenced him to death in absentia. If he ever showed up in Russia again, he was a dead man.

THE SPY WITH ONE HUNDRED FACES

One of Sidney Reilly's fellow spies, and the greatest master of disguise in World War I, was the spy Paul Dukes. His specialty was going undercover in Russia, spying on and sometimes for the Bolsheviks.

SIDNEY'S LUCK RUNS OUT

After the war, Sidney was celebrated by the British for his service and awarded the Military Cross. For a time he lived the life of a celebrity spy. But it didn't last long. He lost money on bad business deals and started asking his spy bosses for money. His bosses got tired of it. They also got tired of Sidney's obsession with the Bolsheviks in Russia. By 1921 the Secret Service had fired him.

Vladimir Lenin led the Russian Revolution in 1917.

By now in the USSR (the union of Russia and other countries under Soviet rule), Lenin was dead and Joseph Stalin had taken his place. Stalin was a ruthless leader who wanted all of the Soviet Union's enemies dead. Sidney was high on Stalin's list. The GPU, Stalin's secret police, set a trap for Sidney. They made up a fake secret group called the Trust, which was purportedly against Stalin. Members of the group contacted Reilly, asking him to join them. Sidney knew there was a risk he was being set up, but he loved taking risks. The GPU arrested Sidney the moment he arrived in the USSR.

No one is sure what happened to Sidney after he was taken prisoner by the GPU. The Bolsheviks said he was killed at the border. Some stories say he was arrested and shot after several days in a Russian prison. One account says that GPU officers killed him in the woods outside of Moscow.

But reports of Sidney sightings continued for years afterward. Though the rumors were probably false, even in death, Sidney's mysteries lived on.

Mata Hari was a world-famous dancer.

CHAPTER 5

MATA HARI: DEADLY SPY OR INNOCENT DANCER?

By the time World War I started, Mata Hari's dancing career was fading. She had been the toast of Europe for years, performing mysterious, enchanting dances for packed theaters. She was beautiful, with long dark hair, dark eyes, and an olive complexion. On stage, she moved with a grace and skill that the newspapers called thrilling, exotic, and daring. Her gem-encrusted costumes entranced audiences everywhere she went.

In 1914, however, her audiences were mostly gone. The world was at war. Mata Hari needed a way to make money to maintain the lavish lifestyle she had grown used to. Could spying be it?

LOCAL GIRL MAKES GOOD

Mata Hari was the stage name for Margaretha Geertruida Zelle, born in Leeuwarden, Netherlands, on August 7, 1876. Her father, a hatmaker, called her his "little princess" and gave her anything she wanted. Life was perfect until she was 13, when her parents divorced. She was sent to live with relatives she hated, and began plotting a way to escape.

When she was 18 years old, the answer came in the newspaper. Margaretha saw an ad from a military officer looking for a wife. Rudolf MacLeod was handsome, smart, an officer, and 39 years old. Four months after they met, Margaretha and Rudolf were married. Soon after, they set sail for the Dutch East Indies

Mati Hari married young as a way to escape from relatives.

(now Indonesia), where Rudolf's company was stationed.

Their marriage was a disaster. Rudolf was an abusive alcoholic who had affairs with other women. Margaretha loved to flirt and enjoyed the company of military officers when Rudolf was away. By 1903 Margaretha and Rudolf were divorced. She traveled to Paris, alone, penniless, and with no way to earn a living.

MATA HARI IS BORN

Margaretha began inventing "holy" and "religious" dances she would later claim she learned in the Indies. She created scandalous costumes that showed off her body. She booked small performances, and soon word spread of the cultured and elegant dancer. Her audiences grew. The only thing she needed was a name that was as exotic as her dancing. She chose Mata Hari, which meant "eye of the day" in Malay, one of the languages of Malaysia.

For the next 10 years she gave sold-out performances all over Europe and became an international celebrity. At the height of her career she made as much as $40,000 for a single performance. And everywhere she went, she met wealthy men who fell in love with her. She spent time with nobility, high-ranking politicians, and military officers from all over Europe. They bought her clothes, jewelry, and apartments, and gave her money to live the lavish lifestyle she loved.

A GERMAN SPY MAKES CONTACT

When World War I broke out in 1914, Mata Hari returned to the Netherlands, but it didn't take long for her to become bored with the quiet life. Her dancing contracts dried up and she needed money. One day someone knocked on her door. Her visitor turned out to be Karl Kroemer, in charge of recruiting spies for Germany. Kroemer asked her to become a German secret agent, for which he would pay her 20,000 francs (about 61,000 U.S. dollars in today's money). He explained to her that her fluency in English, French, Dutch, and German, as well as her connections with French military officers, would be helpful to the German army.

At first Mata Hari said no. It wasn't enough money. Kroemer sweetened the deal by saying it was just a trial. If she did well, she would get more. He gave her the 20,000 francs, three bottles of invisible ink, and the code name "H21."

Did Mata Hari become a German spy that day? Once the money was in her hands, she said she destroyed the invisible ink and never spoke to Kroemer again. There is no evidence that she ever contacted him or spied for the Germans, although she might have passed some rumors to him, knowing they were worthless. But she kept the money.

Mata Hari was still well known, and she didn't try to hide her meeting with Kroemer. It wasn't hard for British spies to quickly find out that Kroemer had tried to recruit Mata Hari. They also knew that she was not married and enjoyed the company of powerful men, at a time when women were expected to be shy and reserved. Her scandalous lifestyle seemed to them a perfect cover for an international spy. So, when Mata Hari left for Paris a few weeks after her meeting with Kroemer, British agents were certain she was off on her first mission. They sent a message to the French secret service. It warned that Mata Hari was a dangerous spy and had to be watched.

MATA HARI, FRENCH SECRET AGENT?

Mata Hari was back in Paris, the City of Light, and loving every minute. What she didn't know was that the French secret service had sent two men, Tartlet and Monier, to follow her. They tracked her every move, stole her mail, and even broke into her rooms and searched for anything that would prove Mata Hari was a spy.

Georges Ladoux, the head of Deuxième Bureau, the French military intelligence agency, was convinced Mata Hari was a German spy. The fact that Tartlet and Monier never found anything didn't slow Ladoux down. It became his mission to find something—anything—to prove she was spying.

Ladoux came up with a plan to trap Mata Hari. He offered her a job as a French undercover agent. She wanted a million francs for the job, and Ladoux agreed, because secretly he never intended to pay her. Their "plan" was for her to infiltrate the highest levels of the German government, even becoming close to Crown Prince Wilhelm. Then she would pass German secrets to Ladoux. Mata Hari still had many male admirers in the German high command, so this idea sounded good.

As Mata Hari prepared to leave for Germany, Ladoux kept surveillance on her mail, phone calls, and everyone she met. He set up the trap even further by contacting the intelligence offices in every country Mata Hari was to travel through, alerting them to the dangerous spy who was on her way.

Mata Hari never made it to Germany. She was detained and searched everywhere she went, just as Ladoux hoped. While stuck in Spain, she met a German officer who gave her some information about the German troops. Frustrated that she couldn't travel to Germany, Mata Hari sent this information back to Ladoux and headed back to Paris. As far as she was concerned, she had done her job and it was time to get paid.

A surprise waited for her in Paris: on February 13, 1917, Mata Hari was arrested as a German spy. Ladoux claimed he'd intercepted several secret German messages about the German spy, "H21," and accused Mata Hari of being that spy. She denied it. But Ladoux had his proof—or so he said.

Mata Hari was convicted as a spy and executed in France on October 15, 1917. To her last day she insisted she was innocent.

INNOCENT OR GUILTY?

Was she, in fact, a secret double agent, blinding her victims with beauty? No one ever found any evidence that she had spied. All of the men who could have spoken in her defense refused to testify at her trial. In any case, everyone was tired of war, and people were ready to hear any news that made them think they were winning. The execution of such an exotic, famous German spy was perfect.

Four days after Mata Hari was executed, Ladoux was arrested as a German spy! His connections in Germany could easily have allowed him to fake the secret German messages about Mata Hari, although no one ever tried to prove it. He was eventually acquitted, but it was the end of his spy career. No one ever trusted him again.

Many years later, the prosecutor in Mata Hari's trial, Andre Mornet, made an astonishing comment. He said of her trial, "There wasn't enough evidence [against her] to flog a cat." Yet he condemned her to death anyway, to serve as an example of what France did to captured German spies.

DID YOU KNOW?

After her death, Mata Hari's head was removed
from her body and given to the Museum of Anatomy,
in Paris. At that time, it was thought that by
studying a criminal's head, science could find
out what caused people to become criminals in the
first place. For years, her mummified head with
its flowing red hair sat in the museum's storage
room, along with more than 5,000 other heads
and body parts. In 2000, the museum began an
inventory of this neglected, grisly collection.
To their shock, Mata Hari's head was gone. No one
knows when it went missing, or who could have
stolen it. Museum officials think the thief was
probably one of her many admirers, who loved her
enough to want a last, macabre reminder of his or
her affection. Her head has never been found.

LEGEND OF THE BEAUTIFUL SPY LIVES ON

Since her death, books, articles, plays, movies, and even ballets have been written about the mysterious Mata Hari. Her name is forever linked with "spy," even though she probably was never a spy at all. The whole truth may never be known.

The mystery around Mata Hari lives on.

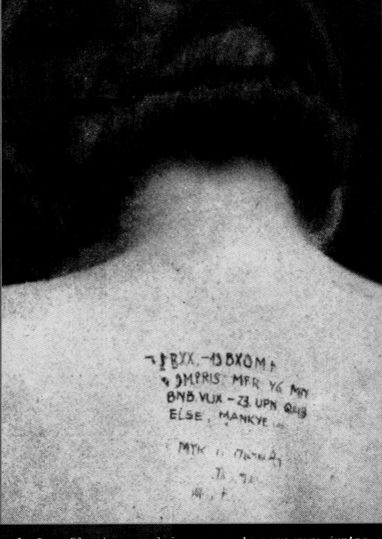

La Dame Blanche smuggled messages in many ways during World War I.

CHAPTER 6

La Dame Blanche: A Network of Spies

A German train rumbled across a lonely stretch of Belgium, carrying supplies to the German troops on the front lines. Miles of empty fields and dark woods stretched in every direction. Small villages dotted the rail line. Near one village, two children played near the train tracks. As the train disappeared in the distance, the children ran to the village and reported to their parents what they had seen: how many cars on the train, and which direction it had been going. The children were spies, part of one of the most secret—and most successful—spy networks of the war.

SECRET EYES ON THE GERMANS

Almost as soon as Germany invaded Belgium in 1914, the German forces took over the entire Belgian railroad system. Soon, huge German supply trains crisscrossed the Belgian tracks on their way to battle. The Allies needed to know everything about those trains. The trains' direction and cargo revealed if they were headed to or from the front lines, and what kinds of supplies were being taken from one area to another. When the Germans moved troops, it was usually because they were getting ready for an attack. But the Allies had no way to send enough spies to Belgium to watch every track. So Mansfield Smith-Cumming, the head of British Intelligence, gave spy Henry Landau a huge mission: find and recruit ordinary Belgian citizens to become train-watching spies for the Allies.

Landau got to work. First he identified the Belgian towns where the trains ran. It was vital that the spies live as close to the train lines as possible. He hired a handful of seasoned agents who had been working for some time. Their mission was to visit the towns and see which local citizens might make good spies. Henry and his partners identified and recruited hundreds of eager Belgian citizens. He named his network of spies "La Dame Blanche," which means "the white lady" in French.

UNDERCOVER TRAINING

Their main spy job was to identify and count the number of German troops, as well as what divisions they were from. If the Allies knew what types of troops and weapons were being transported, they could predict when and where the German army might attack next.

The recruits learned how to recognize different kinds of train transports. For instance, a train carrying troops would have cookers on the back cars. Cavalry trains were filled with horses and horse cars. Artillery trains carried guns on open, flat cars. The new spies were also trained to observe how the troops looked. What age were they? Where they clean? Dirty? How was morale?

New trainees learned how to write their secret reports so no one would find them. The reports were written with a magnifying glass on tiny, thin pieces of tissue paper. Spies used India ink, which would stand up to being wet or damaged. Once the report was written, they learned to roll it so that it was very tiny and could be hidden almost anywhere.

SMUGGLING SECRET REPORTS

The spies of the White Lady had one mission: watch German troop movements along the railroads and make daily or weekly reports.

They needed a safe and secret way to pass along their messages, and they couldn't know one another's identities. Landau had a name for the sneaky spy system he invented to solve this problem: the "octopus" system. One agent, the Letterbox, who lived in town and received the messages, was the body of the octopus. The field agents in that town were the tentacles. They passed their reports to the Letterbox, but only if it was safe. The agents used secret signs that no one else knew. For instance, a flowerpot in a certain position, or a curtain pulled up or down signaled "safe" or "not safe."

The agents had many smart ways to smuggle their messages. They sewed them into their clothing. They hid them in hollow basket handles. Tin boxes with false bottoms worked especially well. They put their messages in bars of soap or in fresh vegetables. Women hid messages in their hair.

The Letterbox agent collected the reports, checked them, and then gave them to the passeur, or ferryman, who smuggled them to the Allies. This was an especially dangerous job since the Germans had built a 10-foot-tall (3-meter-tall) electric fence along the border. German patrols guarded the fence every 100 yards (91 meters). Passeurs snuck to the fence at night, dodging the lights and guards. Sometimes they waited for days, hidden, until they saw a chance to slip through.

Passeurs used thick rubber gloves to get through the fence. Sometimes they used a barrel with no top or bottom to shove between the electric wires, allowing them to crawl through the fence. Volunteering to be a passeur was not for the weak of heart. More than 3,000 passeurs were electrocuted during the war.

As the war dragged on, the Germans figured out they were being spied on. So they tried to confuse the spies by removing all the badges and insignia from their uniforms. This way, the spies wouldn't be able to identify the German troops. At first the trick worked. Then Landau got an idea. He recruited hundreds of new agents, called pomeneures, or walkers. Their job was to go undercover as regular citizens and

DID YOU KNOW?

Almost 75 percent of the intelligence
from all German occupied areas came from
White Lady agents.

SECRET AGENT, SECRET PROMISE

Every La Dame Blanche agent swore an oath, promising to
do their duty for their country:

*I declare and enlist in the capacity of soldier in the Allied
military observation service until the end of the war. I
swear before God to respect this engagement, to accomplish
conscientiously the offices entrusted to me, to comply
with the instructions given to me by the representatives
of the Direction, not to reveal to anyone (without formal
authorization) anything concerning the organization
of the service, even if this stance should entail for me or
mine the penalty of death, not to take part in any other
activity or role that might expose me to prosecution by the
occupying authority.*

make friendly conversation with the German soldiers when the trains stopped at rest areas. By mingling and talking directly to the troops, the spies could find out what divisions they were from and where they were headed. No German army ever got past La Dame Blanche without being identified.

DANGEROUS WORK

A spy for La Dame Blanche could be anyone. Men, women, and children worked as agents. They were nuns, priests, bankers, teachers, artists, and businessmen. Many of the White Lady spy teams were families. Anna Kesseler and her four daughters joined and worked as couriers and Letterboxes.

The Latouche family was one of the best of these teams. The father (a former railroad worker), mother, and two teenage daughters developed a schedule so the daughters kept watch during the day and the parents took over at night. To avoid getting caught, the family wrote all their reports in code, making their notes look like a grocery list. They used beans to tell the number of German soldiers, chicory for the number of horses, and coffee beans for the number of enemy cannons. They hid their lists in hollow broom handles.

In the Arnold family, 13-year-old Gerardine and her little brother would "play" on the railroad tracks so they could report everything they saw. If visitors came to the house, the children took over watch duties while their parents were busy.

Train-watching work could be boring and lonely. Railroad tracks had to be watched day and night. One agent, Julie Barnich, watched trains with her brother Adolphe. She wrote, "There is nothing more horrible than long winter nights in a room without light in forced idleness . . . fighting drowsiness and fearing to fail in one's duty. The next day, taking up the same life, with nothing, not relaxation, nor distraction to come break the somber monotony of the existence."

AT WAR'S END

The White Lady spy network was one of the most successful networks of the war. In 1918 alone, the network provided Allied troops with hundreds of pounds of notes, reports, and maps of German troop movements. Because of the White Lady network, the Allies knew exactly where the Germans were every day.

When the war ended, La Dame Blanche spies got something that few wartime spies received: recognition. Each received a certificate of honor and the grateful thanks of both Britain and Belgium.

SPIES!

FEARLESS SPIES AND DARING DEEDS OF WORLD WAR II

Germany was in a tough position after losing World War I. The country was forced to pay large sums of money to the victors, and its national boundaries were redrawn. This led to an economic depression in Germany that paved the way for a person with big promises. His campaign slogan was "freedom and bread" for everyone—what he had in mind was something quite different.

In 1933, Hitler was appointed chancellor of Germany. Soon after, he overturned the democratic system there to become the Führer, or absolute ruler, of Germany. He and his National Socialist German Workers' Party, known as Nazis, at first enjoyed broad support, both domestically and internationally. However, it wasn't long before the world learned the truth: Hitler hoped to take over most of Europe and create an "Aryan," or superior, race by wiping out minority populations. Hitler wanted to rid the world of Jewish people, Romas, homosexuals, the disabled, and others who did not fit his idea of perfection. Many in Europe and the United States became increasingly alarmed.

World War II started in Europe after Hitler's invasion of Poland on September 1, 1939. Two days later, Great Britain and France declared war on Germany. During the course of the war, more than 30 countries took sides. The two sides were called the Allies and the Axis. The Allies included Great Britain, France, the Soviet Union, and the United States. The Axis powers included Germany, Italy, and Japan.

The United States had sympathized with the Allies but stayed out of the war until Japan attacked Pearl Harbor in Hawaii on December 7, 1941. Japan had been trying to take over parts of Asia for many years, and the United States opposed their movements toward expanding. War felt imminent, but still, the attack on Pearl Harbor took the United States by surprise. About 3,500 Americans were wounded or killed during the attack.

In the spring of 1945, Germany's forces faced defeat. Hitler, knowing he had lost the war, committed suicide on April 30, 1945.
On May 7, 1945, Germany surrendered to the Allies. Japan surrendered on September 2, 1945, after the U.S. military dropped atomic bombs on Hiroshima and Nagasaki.

More than 60 million soldiers and civilians died during the war. The actions of spies on both sides influenced and, in some cases, changed the course of the war. This section tells the stories of the daring deeds of some of these fearless spies.

Krystyna Skarbek, alias Christine Granville,
was a fearless spy.

CHAPTER 7

CHRISTINE GRANVILLE: BRITAIN'S BEAUTY QUEEN SPY

As Count and Countess Skarbek of Poland leaned over their newborn's crib in 1908, they no doubt imagined a bright future for their little Krystyna. She would one day make her debut in Polish society, catch the eye of a young aristocrat, and raise children with royal titles.

But this was not to be. By the time she was a teen, the count and countess's spirited daughter was kicked out of one boarding school after another for not following rules. Krystyna attended Catholic schools and found the schools' required religious instruction boring. One time she even tried to liven up mass by setting the priest's robes on fire.

School wasn't all bad, though. Krystyna enjoyed sports and languages, especially French. Her athletic ability and knack for languages were to prove very useful in Krystyna's adult life. Around the time Krystyna's schoolgirl days ended so did her family's good fortune. The family bank went out of business and the Skarbeks were forced to sell their country estate. Worse, Count Skarbek deserted his family, leaving them to fend for themselves in the cramped city apartment to which they had to move.

Now in her 20s, and not the type of person to wait for someone to rescue her, Krystyna found a job at a car dealership to support herself. She also submitted her photograph to a local newspaper for the Miss Poland beauty contest. As a runner-up, she earned the title "Star of Beauty." But as beautiful as she was on the outside, her insides were becoming damaged from breathing the exhaust fumes at the car dealership. After taking X-rays, doctors warned that her lungs were permanently scarred. They suggested she needed clean mountain air to recuperate.

Krystyna found both clean air and a husband in Zakopane, a ski town. Jerzy Gizycki caught her as she tumbled in a skiing accident. Several years her senior, Jerzy worked for the Polish Foreign Office and was a world traveler.

VOLUNTEER SPY

In August 1939 Krystyna's husband was directed to open a consulate in the British Colony of Kenya. Jerzy and Krystyna packed up their belongings and traveled by ship to South Africa. From there, they would make the long drive north to Kenya. But within days of landing in Africa, they heard the devastating news that under Adolf Hitler's command, the German army had invaded Poland on September 1, 1939. Not long after, on September 17, the Soviet Army, in alliance with the Germans, invaded Poland as well.

On September 1, 1939, Germany invaded Poland.

As a result, not only would there be no Kenyan consulate, the future of Poland itself was unsure. Krystyna and Jerzy decided to go to Great Britain and volunteer to help with the war effort.

Within a few weeks of arriving in Britain, Krystyna found the offices for the British Secret Intelligence Services (SIS). She marched in and volunteered to spy behind enemy lines for the

Special Operations Executive (SOE). At first the SOE thought Krystyna Skarbek Gizycki might be crazy. Walk-ins often were, and her plan certainly sounded crazy. She had volunteered to ski from Hungary past the German patrol guarding the Polish border. Then, in occupied Poland, she would meet with members of the Polish Resistance and deliver and carry intelligence reports.

SOE intelligence officers were torn over whether to accept Krystyna's offer. She had the language skills, athletic ability, and personal contacts in Poland to be a valuable agent. But did she have the right temperament? Did she have the courage and intellect to succeed in the life-or-death stakes a spy would face? Krystyna's charm and fierce national pride eventually won them over. She was commissioned to be a spy for Britain, and was given the first in a string of several false identities. Her best-known identity was Christine Granville.

After a small amount of intelligence training, she boarded a train for Budapest, Hungary, to await orders to proceed. When the approval came to go forward, it was the dead of winter. Temperatures dipped to minus 22 degrees Fahrenheit (minus 30 degrees Celsius). Christine made contact with a professional skier aligned with the Resistance and arranged for him to act as her guide. The two of them boarded a train headed for Czechoslovakia.

DID YOU KNOW?

During World War II, the countries
involved aligned into two groups: the
Allies and the Axis. The Allies were at
first composed of France, Poland, and
Great Britain. Later the United States,
the Soviet Union, China, Canada,
Australia, New Zealand, Belgium, and
other countries joined.

The Axis side included Germany, Japan,
and Italy, with Bulgaria, Hungary,
Romania, and Thailand later joining.

They jumped out while the train was moving to avoid detection at the border checkpoint. They skied and hiked toward Poland for days. One night during a blizzard they slept in a hunting shack. Even above the howling blizzard they heard screaming but they could see nothing outside. The next morning Christine found two frozen bodies. They later learned that thirty Polish people had frozen to death near their hut that night trying to escape from the Germans.

After finally arriving in German-occupied Poland, Christine met with Resistance leaders. She brought them British propaganda to copy and distribute. Even as the Germans imposed their brutal domination over Poland, forcing Jewish people into ghettos and publicly executing dissenters, Christine organized underground radio broadcasts. She also collected information to send to Britain.

Each time she traveled she faced the danger of being searched. If the documents from the Polish Resistance were found, she would be executed, but Christine always had a plan. Once, the naturally friendly and attractive spy struck up a conversation with a German officer on a train. After cozying up to him she whispered that she was carrying a packet of black market tea for her sick mother. Could he be a dear and carry it for her? In this way she tricked more than one unsuspecting German soldier into carrying her documents for her.

FAST TALKER

She wasn't always so lucky. On one trip she and a member of the Polish Resistance were arrested at a train depot. The local police thought it was suspicious for her and her companion to be waiting at a deserted depot at night. As they were marched over a bridge toward Gestapo headquarters for questioning, the spies dropped their secret documents into the river below. Furious, the local police confiscated the rest of their belongings, including their ID cards. They discovered Christine's stash of money and had begun dividing it between them when they noticed her necklace. Though it was only glass, Christine pretended the necklace was made of diamonds and begged them not to take it. The greedy officers fought over it, allowing Christine and her companion to escape. Afterward, Christine's ID containing her "Miss Poland" photo was posted in every train station offering a reward for her capture.

In other ways, Christine's work became more dangerous than ever. Her home base in Hungary posed new dangers after the country sided with Germany in the war. As a result, Christine and another spy were arrested at Christine's apartment in Budapest on suspicion of spying. Christine endured two days of interrogation and beatings. Sick with the flu and exhausted, Christine devised a plan to trick them into letting her go. She coughed furiously and bit her tongue so it looked as though she had coughed up blood.

She claimed she was being treated for tuberculosis (TB), a highly contagious disease affecting the lungs. A doctor ordered an X-ray, and because her lungs had been scarred years ago from car exhaust fumes, it seemed she really did have TB. No one, including the Gestapo officers, wanted to get the disease, so they set her free along with her partner, whom they suspected might be carrying the disease as well. After Christine and her partner were sent back to her apartment, they escaped from Hungary.

With her cover blown in both Poland and Hungary, Christine was reassigned to Cairo. There she received additional spy training. She was eventually selected for one of the most

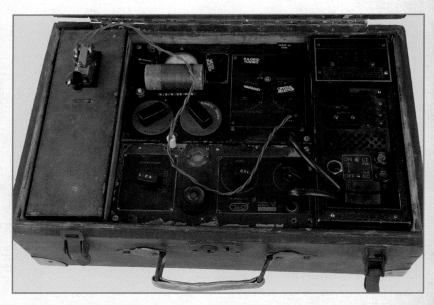

Christine used a radio like this one to transmit messages to the Allies.

dangerous World War II spy assignments: radio transmitter. The life expectancy of a radio transmitter behind enemy lines was six weeks. The woman Christine replaced had been captured, tortured, and executed. After training, Christine parachuted into occupied France in 1944 with a knife strapped to her thigh and a rubber-encased suicide pill sewn into her clothing.

Part of her new assignment was to work with fellow SOE agent Francis Cammaerts watching for midnight parachute drops from the Allies. They would race to pick up the dropped ammunition and supplies and then store them in Resistance safe houses.

After one run, Francis and two other spies were stopped by the Gestapo. Upon searching them, the German officers became suspicious when they realized all the spies' money had consecutive serial numbers. Consecutive serial numbers most likely meant they received the money from a central source, which made it look like counterfeit money. So, the Gestapo believed them to be spies. They were arrested and taken to a makeshift prison. Their execution was scheduled for three days later on August 17, 1944, at 9:00 p.m.

Christine biked 25 miles (40 kilometers) to the prison and slipped inside with visitors. She promised an officer there that she would bring him money if he arranged a meeting with the arresting officer. When she returned two days later with the cash, the Allied forces had arrived in France and were quickly advancing. It appeared the war was about to end.

When she finally met with the arresting officer, Christine broke the first rule of spying, just as she had broken rules in school. She admitted she was a British wireless transmitter. She pulled two broken transmitter crystals out of her pocket to prove it. Then she spun horrific stories of what the advancing Allies planned to do with captured Nazis. She convinced the officer that, since he was Belgian, his homeland would execute him as a traitor. Only by releasing her fellow spies could she guarantee his safety.

THE RESISTANCE

Resistance is the term used to describe a secret or underground group that opposes the rule forced on them. During World War II when France was occupied by Germany, the French Resistance, including a group known as the *Maquis* that Christine Granville worked with, did much to thwart Germany. Resistance members were often loosely organized, and their activities ranged from publishing propaganda, hiding supplies and spies, evacuating Jewish people, sabotaging enemy communications and supplies, and assassinating enemy forces.

Two hours before their scheduled execution, Francis and the other two spies walked out of prison, thanks to a rule-breaking beauty queen.

Francis Cammaerts (left) attended Christine's funeral.

Captain Ewen Montagu and his colleagues came up with the idea behind Operation Mincemeat.

CHAPTER 8

WILLIAM MARTIN: OPERATION MINCEMEAT'S COOL SPY ON ICE

In April 1943, Major William Martin of the Royal Marines was dressed, packed, and prepared for his first and only spy mission. His job was to leak false information to the Germans. He had to convince them the Allies would land in Greece or the Italian island of Sardinia rather than their real target: Sicily. A large island located at off the tip of Italy, Sicily was an ideal landing spot for an invasion, but the Germans knew that and were already prepared for an Allied invasion there. If Martin's mission was successful, the Germans would divert their troops to Greece and Sardinia, leaving Sicily poorly defended. Then the Allies could land and launch a ground attack there.

Major Martin's assignment was a delicate one. He would have to be shipwrecked and captured by the enemy, allowing them to seize his false documents. He would have to play his part flawlessly. But even though it was Martin's first espionage assignment, he wasn't the least bit nervous. In fact, he had no feelings about the mission at all, as Major Martin was quite dead.

Major Martin was drafted into service by Captain Ewen Montagu and his colleagues at the British Special Operations Executive. The operation for which he was drafted was called Operation Mincemeat. Ian Fleming, an SOE agent and later the creator of the James Bond, 007 character, came up with the idea along with other creative SOE agents. They wanted to create the illusion that Major Martin was on a secret mission to deliver important papers when his military plane crashed and he was shipwrecked in the ocean. The SOE would make it look as though he had drowned and his body and briefcase floated ashore. It was certainly a plot worthy of a James Bond movie.

Montagu and his colleagues first had to convince their superiors the plan would work. Winston Churchill, the British prime minister, said they had "corkscrew minds," but ultimately they were given the go-ahead. Their biggest challenge lay in finding a dead body that no one would miss. And not just any body would do. The age had to be right for military service and the cause of death had to appear to be drowning. With some help from the local coroner they found an appropriate candidate. He was given the name Major William Martin because it was a common last name among British Royal Marines. Though many theories have sprung up about his real identity, it has never been officially revealed.

Ian Fleming, the creator of James Bond, helped conceive Operation Mincemeat.

OPERATION GREIF

The Germans had a few tricks up their sleeves when it came to imposters and disinformation too. They launched Operation Greif in December of 1944. They selected German soldiers who spoke English and dressed them in military uniforms belonging to captured U.S. servicemen. The imposters infiltrated U.S. units during the Battle of the Bulge and began causing chaos. They moved traffic signs, destroyed ammunition, and cut communication lines.

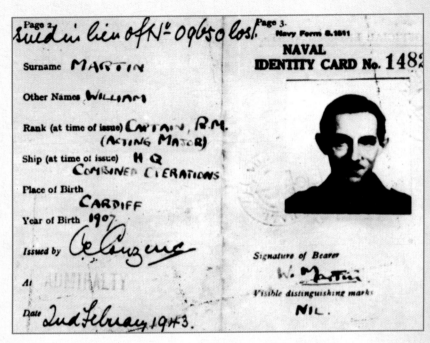

Page 2.
Sudin lien of N° 09650 lost.

Page 3.
Navy Form S.1811

NAVAL
IDENTITY CARD No. 148?

Surname *MARTIN*

Other Names *WILLIAM*

Rank (at time of issue) *CAPTAIN, R.M.*
(ACTING MAJOR)

Ship (at time of issue) *H Q*
COMBINED OPERATIONS

Place of Birth
CARDIFF

Year of Birth *1907*

Issued by *(signature)*

At *ADMIRALTY*

Date *2nd February 1943.*

Signature of Bearer
W. Martin

Visible distinguishing marks
NIL.

William Martin's identification papers

The SOE office created false identity papers and military records
for Major Martin using photographs of an employee who resembled
Martin. They carefully forged official-looking correspondence from
one general to another hinting at the Allies' landing in Sardinia.
These documents were to appear so important that the major had
to deliver them personally in a briefcase chained to his wrist.

DID YOU KNOW?

Ian Fleming wasn't the only spy to
write blockbuster spy novels. David
John Moore Cornwell, better known by
his pen name, John Le Carré, worked in
British foreign intelligence during the
Cold War. He wrote many best-selling
spy books, including *The Spy Who Came
in from the Cold* and *Tinker Tailor
Soldier Spy*, which were later turned
into movies.

POCKET LITTER

Worried that the Germans might figure out their scheme, Montagu's team had to make absolutely certain that their fake spy was believable. They created everyday items that spies call "pocket litter" for Martin to carry in his coat pocket and wallet to make him appear genuine: ticket stubs from a play, receipts, and money, as well as keys and matches. The major also carried love letters and a snapshot of his "fiancée" wearing a bathing suit. Montagu even made the documents appear worn out by rubbing them against his leg and folding and refolding them over and over.

The body was refrigerated until the operation started. Then it was wrapped in a blanket to avoid damage, placed in a metal tube filled with dry ice, and taken aboard a Royal Navy submarine. The briefcase with documents was looped through Major Martin's coat and attached to his wrist. A life preserver was strapped to his chest. An officer read the 39th Psalm and the crew prayed over Major Martin before committing his body to the sea. A damaged rubber dinghy was also dropped in the water off the coast of Spain under the cover of darkness on April 30, 1943. Spain was officially neutral, but its government was friendly toward Germany. The SOE believed any Spaniard who spotted a body in a British Naval uniform would report it to police, who would, in turn, report it to the Germans.

A Spanish fisherman near Huelva, Spain, spotted the body and alerted the police. Just as the British had predicted, Major Martin and his "secrets" were turned over to the Germans. After the Germans read the documents, they resealed them, placed them back in the briefcase, and the Spanish police turned Major Martin's body over to the British. He received a military funeral with full honors and was buried in Spain.

Meanwhile, the Germans couldn't believe their luck! They fell for the scheme and routed many of their troops and tanks to Sardinia and Greece to fight the Allies when they landed. But the Allies landed in Sicily, just as they had always planned, on July 10, 1943. With German forces stretched thin to cover Sardinia and Greece, the Allies faced much less resistance in Sicily owing to the work of an anonymous dead spy.

The Allies invaded Sicily, Italy, in 1943.

William Sebold (left) was a double-agent spy.

CHAPTER 9

WILLIAM SEBOLD: AMERICA'S NERVOUS BUT PATRIOTIC SPY

William Sebold was born a German, but later chose to become a U.S. citizen. Born in 1899 as Wilhelm Sebold, he fought for Germany in World War I, which led to injuries that would bother him throughout his life.

After the war, he wandered from one job to another and through several countries. He settled for a time in the Yorkville section of New York City, which was home to many German immigrants. He married the daughter of German immigrants and became a U.S. citizen in February 1936.

Nervous by nature and constantly sick with stomach problems from his exposure to mustard gas in the war, William required surgery to repair stomach ulcers. He and his wife separated during this time, leaving a weak and sick William all alone. Despite the fact that Germany was on the brink of another war, William returned there to recuperate at his mother's home in February 1939.

As required by law, when William arrived in Germany he reported to the passport office. He was interrogated about his activities in the United States and then told that the police would be in touch with him. A few months later, a man named Dr. Gassner showed up at his mother's house. Gassner said the Germans wanted him to work for them when he returned to America. William wasn't interested, but Gassner threatened to report that William had lied on his American citizenship application, failing to reveal his time served in a German jail. Gassner gave him a month to decide. Fearing for both his life and his mother's life if he refused, Sebold agreed, even while his loyalty lay with America.

William was trained to send messages using Morse code and a coding system using pages from a popular novel. He learned about microphotography and microdots, which shrank pictures and words, making them visible only with a magnifying lens.

While William was in Germany, his American passport was stolen. He reported it to the U.S. consulate and took the opportunity to tell the staff he had been blackmailed into spying for the Germans, but was loyal to the United States. Could the United States help him? U.S. officials recorded his information but were skeptical.

William continued his German spy training with a heavy heart. After a brief hospitalization for his nerves, the Germans gave him U.S. currency and names of contacts in the United States. They ordered him to purchase a special camera for microphotography and a radio device to send and receive transmissions once he was back in America. They gave him a code name—Harry Sawyer—and sent him to New York.

AMERICAN SPY

With his new marching orders, William was sent back to his adopted American homeland aboard the USS *Washington* in February 1940. When he arrived in America, two Federal Bureau of Investigation (FBI) agents met him. It was the first sign William had that his request at the consulate had been taken seriously. The FBI offered him a job as a double agent at a salary of $50 a month.

The FBI set up radio transmitter equipment for William. They assigned an FBI agent to listen to the transmissions. William made contact with the names given to him while FBI agents listened. Before long a whole team of FBI agents were following German spies.

William's German spy duties included receiving packets of money from a contact who worked aboard a ship that made stops in both Germany and New York. William acted as the paymaster, using the money to pay some of his fellow German spies in the United States. Before long, travel between the countries became difficult because of the war, so a new method of payment was needed. His German handlers radioed a message directing William to set up a business where they could transfer money to him directly without arousing suspicion.

TRAPPING SPIES

The FBI was overjoyed—this would bring the German spies straight into their trap! They set up his business office in Times Square. The office of William G. Sebold, diesel engineer, was equipped with the latest hidden audio- and video-recording devices. The FBI set up its offices next door. Through a two-way mirror, they could watch and record William's meetings with his German spy network. Best of all, the Germans unknowingly footed the bill for it all.

Spies came and went from the Times Square office. Film rolled night and day. And hundreds of radio messages were received and sent. William, though generally nervous and panicky, did surprisingly well with the support of the FBI. It was the biggest operation in FBI history at the time. After several months of surveillance, the FBI arrested 33 men and women. Twenty-eight were born in Germany, of whom 22 had become naturalized American citizens. Others were from Latvia, France, and South Africa. The newspapers dubbed them the Duquesne Spy Ring, named for one of the better-known spies, Fritz Duquesne.

DID YOU KNOW?

Some of the spies in the Duquesne
Spy Ring were involved in industrial
espionage: spying on corporations
that provided the military with goods
and services. This allowed them to
photograph and report back on new or
improved weaponry, steal operation
manuals, and anticipate how many
weapons and goods the United States
would manufacture.

FRITZ DUQUESNE

Fritz Duquesne, for whom the Duquesne Spy Ring was named, had been a noted big game hunter in South Africa. He fought for the South African Republic against the British in the Second Boer War (1899–1902), where his life as a spy began. As a spy, he infiltrated the British army and posed as an officer to sabotage their missions. He spied for the Germans during both world wars. He tried unsuccessfully to assassinate British military commander Lord Horatio Herbert Kitchener. For this he was imprisoned in a British jail in Bermuda. He escaped and came to New York. In the United States he worked as an adventure journalist writing about safari hunting and even became President Theodore Roosevelt's shooting instructor. He then worked as a movie publicist for RKO Pictures and lectured about big game hunting.

William Sebold (left) would have conversations with Duquesne and tape them for the FBI.

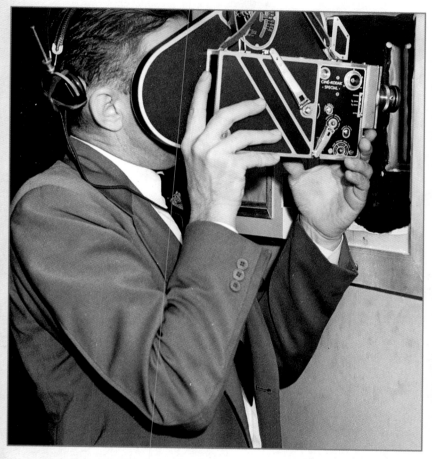

William Sebold helped the FBI film suspected spies.

Faced with the knowledge they had been followed and recorded, many of the spies pleaded guilty. The trial for the 14 who held out began in September 1941, with William Sebold as the star witness for the prosecution.

The events that took place during the three-month trial did little to benefit the defense. Although the United States had not yet entered World War II, their ships helped escort and protect other countries' ships. The USS *Reuben James* was torpedoed and sunk by German submarines on October 31, 1941, making it the first U.S. war casualty. Five weeks later, the Japanese bombed Pearl Harbor on December 7, 1941. Germany declared war on the United States on December 11, 1941. In return, the United States declared war on Japan December 8 and on Germany December 11.

On December 13, 1941, the jury deliberated until close to midnight before finding all the defendants guilty. They received sentences ranging from a few months to several years. William Sebold had taken down a huge German spy ring before the United States had even entered the war. In gratitude for his patriotic service, he was secretly relocated to Walnut Creek, California, outside San Francisco to start a new life, courtesy of the FBI.

THE
33 CONVICTED MEMBERS
OF THE
DUQUESNE
SPY RING

William helped expose the Duquesne Spy Ring.

Richard Sakakida, while stationed in the Philippines

CHAPTER 10

RICHARD SAKAKIDA: THE SPY WHO NEEDED HIS MOM'S PERMISSION

Born in Hawaii to Japanese immigrants, Richard Sakakida dreamed of life on the mainland beyond the Hawaiian Islands. He worked hard in high school, trained in the ROTC, and studied his mother's native tongue at Japanese language school in the afternoons. After graduation he worked two jobs, one at a furniture company and the other as an announcer at a Japanese language radio station. Each week he gave his earnings to his mother to help with family expenses. But Richard wanted more out of life.

When his former high school ROTC instructor arranged a job interview for him involving travel, Richard jumped at the chance. The interview lasted an entire day. He and 30 other young Japanese-American men were questioned by military officers and tested on their Japanese-to-English translation skills.

Richard Sakakida and Arthur Komori were both chosen for the job. It wasn't until after Richard accepted the job that he was informed he would be a special intelligence agent for the army's Counter Intelligence Corps (CIC). There was just one catch. In 1941 army recruits under the age of 21 had to have a parent's signature to enlist. Richard, then 20 years old, may be the only spy in history whose mother had to sign his permission slip.

Richard's dream of travel didn't unfold as he anticipated. He thought he would be taken to the U.S. mainland for intelligence training. Instead he and Komori were shipped to the Philippines. Richard's secret life began the day he boarded the ship. Though surrounded by other U.S. armed forces members also commissioned to serve in the Philippines, Richard wasn't allowed to speak to any of them so as not to blow his cover. He had to pose as a member of the ship's crew. When the ship docked, Richard was given a packet of information by one of the ship's officers telling him where to report.

Following orders, Richard parted ways with Komori and checked into the Japanese-owned Nishikawa hotel in Manila. He met his contact, Major Raymond, in front of city hall a few nights later. Given the code name Sixto Borja, he was told to check a post office box daily for directions. In order to gather intelligence on local Japanese businessmen suspected of gathering U.S. military information, he needed a cover. Pretending to be a Japanese citizen, he took a retail job at a store during the day. In the evenings he worked the desk at the Nishikawa hotel. This gave him access to the

Japanese guests' passports and personal information.

When Japan bombed Pearl Harbor in Richard's native Hawaii on December 7, 1941, it plunged the Philippines into turmoil. The Philippine government ordered all Japanese nationals in Manila to be interned at the Nippon Club, a social club for Japanese businessmen. Although Richard was only posing as a Japanese national, Major Raymond told him to keep his cover with the Japanese and gather intelligence. So Richard reported with his fellow hotel guests as directed. He stayed until two American intelligence agents got him out by posing as military police and pretending to arrest him.

Hours after bombing Pearl Harbor, the Japanese also bombed

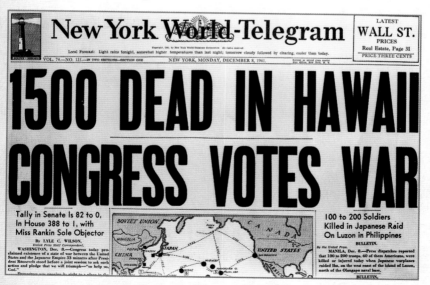

The Japanese bombing of Pearl Harbor on December 7, 1941, brought the United States into World War II.

U.S. military targets in the Philippines and soon invaded the area. As the Japanese army advanced, Richard had to stay ahead of them. He worked in Fort Santiago before moving to Bataan and then Corregidor, broadcasting American propaganda in Japanese, intercepting radio transmissions, translating enemy communications, and interrogating Japanese prisoners. He and Komori worked virtually around the clock, sleeping at their desks and living off ever-dwindling rations.

Shortly after Richard evacuated Bataan, it fell under Japanese control. More than 70,000 American and Filipino prisoners of war were forced to march many miles north to prison camps. Thousands died of injuries, starvation, and dysentery during the Bataan Death March. The island of Corregidor, to where Richard had relocated, couldn't hold out much longer. Richard and Komori were offered seats on an evacuation plane headed for Australia. But Richard gave his spot to another man and stayed to work as a translator for General Beebe and General Wainwright during the U.S. surrender of the island of Corregidor.

During surrender talks with the Japanese, Richard was introduced as a civilian translator, but the Japanese quickly identified him as the American voice on the radio. They would not allow him to translate for the United States. In retaliation for his lie, a Japanese officer punched him in the face and shattered his glasses. Richard wasn't able to see clearly again until after the war.

DID YOU KNOW?

In the years just before World War II, the
Philippines, an area of more than 7,000
islands, was under the command of the United
States. The United States operated several
military bases there, making it a tempting
target for Japanese aggression. The Japanese
battled against the Americans, Australians,
British, and Philippine nationals for control
of the area known as the South West Pacific
Theater. The area included the Philippines,
Dutch East Indies, Borneo, Australia, New
Guinea, and the Solomon Islands.

UNDER ARREST

Immediately following the surrender Richard was imprisoned by the Japanese, placed in a tiny cell, and given little to eat. Suspecting he was not only military, but in intelligence as well, they interrogated him around the clock for months. Richard insisted he was a civilian working as a translator. Although he was a U.S. citizen by birth, his Japanese captors charged him with treason, stating he was a dual citizen of both America and Japan, and was therefore a traitor to his Japanese homeland.

When interrogation didn't work, Richard was tortured day after day to confess. He was bound with rope and hung from the ceiling rafters until the bones in his arms and shoulders were dislocated. Despite being stripped and burned with cigarettes he never wavered from his story.

Eventually he was cleared of the treason charge when the Japanese discovered that although Mrs. Sakakida had originally registered her son as a dual citizen, she had renounced her son's Japanese citizenship before his twenty-first birthday. Richard lied to his captors, claiming his mother had done so because she had disowned him when he left Hawaii. In reality, she had probably been advised by his commanding officer to do so.

The Japanese captured prisoners and took them on what came to be known as the Bataan Death March.

UNDERCOVER SPY ONCE MORE

With no confession, no treason charge, and no proof he was military, the Japanese decided Richard was probably harmless. But he possessed language skills they wanted to use, so they transferred him to the personal service of Japanese Colonel Nishiharu. Richard became his assistant and worked at his office. Before long he was back to spying. He copied, logged, and filed incoming documents. He now had access to valuable information, but no way to pass it along to the U.S. military. He solved that problem when Mrs. Tupas, the wife of an imprisoned Filipino Resistance fighter named Ernest Tupas, came to the office seeking a pass to visit her husband in jail. Richard supplied her with a steady stream of stolen visitor passes and special authorizations to bring food packages into the prison. This allowed her to visit her husband and carry both Richard's messages and tools for a prison breakout.

During October 1943 Richard, along with members of the Filipino Resistance, dressed in Japanese uniforms, entered the Mantinlupa prison and disarmed the guards. Meanwhile, Ernest Tupas, who worked in the prison power plant, shut down the electrical system, allowing hundreds of political prisoners to escape. Once Tupas was on the outside he arranged telegraphs to U.S. General Douglas MacArthur's Australian headquarters, reporting Japanese troop movements and shipping information from Richard.

Despite having arranged the breakout of hundreds of Filipino prisoners, Richard remained a prisoner himself. As the war began to turn in the Americans' favor, Richard planned his escape. He hid pouches of rice, a mess kit, a knife, and even a stolen gun and ammunition. When the colonel and his staff evacuated, Richard claimed he was too ill to move, but would catch up with them.

He hid in the jungle, living on rice, jungle fruits, and grass. Japanese and American artillery shells rained down all around him. Richard was hit in the stomach with shrapnel and had to use a razor to cut the metal fragments out of his abdomen. Malnourished and delirious with infection from performing surgery on himself, he wandered the jungle for nearly five months. Overhearing two men speaking English, a frail, dazed Richard emerged from the jungle with his hands up. "Don't shoot. I'm an American!" he yelled.

The war had been over for weeks, with the Americans victorious. But before being taken to a hospital to recuperate, the young spy Richard Sakakida had unfinished business to attend to. Richard had to call his mother.

HIROO ONODA

Richard Sakakida wasn't the only spy to wander the Philippine jungle after the war ended. The world record probably goes to Hiroo Onoda. Onoda was a Japanese intelligence officer, who, near the end of the war, hid in the jungle. Upon hearing of Japan's defeat, Onoda decided it was a trick. For 29 years he lived in the jungle, eating berries and

food he stole from nearby farmers. All the while he refused to believe Japan had lost the war. Finally, in 1974, he came out of hiding. Dressed in his ragged military uniform, Onoda presented his sword to his former commanding officer. He returned to Japan as a hero.

Hiroo Onoda refused to believe that Japan surrendered.

Claus Schenk Graf von Stauffenberg,
plotted against Hitler.

CHAPTER 11

CLAUS SCHENK GRAF VON STAUFFENBERG: OPERATION VALKYRIE'S THREE-FINGERED SPY

Count Alfred von Stauffenberg did not think his youngest son's decision to join the Cavalry Regiment of the German army in April 1926, was a wise choice. A career in the army was so beneath him, so lower-class. Men did not make a name for themselves in the army. Before the German Revolution of 1918, which had abolished royal rule and noble titles, the elder von Stauffenberg had served the king of Wurttemberg (an area of old Germany) as Lord Chamberlain. Little did the count know that his son's name would one day be infamous.

Claus did well in the army. He was an excellent horseman, proud German, and quick thinker. In 1936 he graduated from cavalry horses to tanks and motorcycles in the elite Berlin War Academy. There he met other young men from aristocratic families in a group called the Kreisau Circle. They discussed politics and ideals at their meetings. He was a rising star, first in his class, and moving steadily up the ladder of military success.

Though Claus was a patriotic German, he, like some other members of the Kreisau Circle, became disillusioned with Hitler's politics. Claus privately expressed disgust over the 1938 Kristallnacht, the Night of Broken Glass, in which Jewish-owned businesses were looted. Synagogues were burned, and thousands of Jewish men and boys were beaten, rounded up, and forced into concentration camps. Claus was a nationalist. He believed in Germany's right to wage war and wanted, above all, for Germany to be victorious. However, he hated the increasing brutality of the Nazi party. As the war progressed, he frequently questioned the tactical ability of the Führer, as Hitler was known. The Germans lost hundreds of thousands of soldiers in Stalingrad before finally surrendering the area on February 2, 1943. Claus von Stauffenberg knew then that something must be done about Adolf Hitler.

Claus was not alone in questioning his commander's ability. Several members of the army shared his views, including some of his old friends from the Kreisau Circle. But Claus had little time for such thoughts. He was sent to the African front to serve in Tunis, Tunisia the same month, February 1943. Two months later, on April 7, Claus's vehicle was hit by American bombers. Claus lost his left eye and had his right hand amputated as well as two fingers from his left hand. For the rest of his life he wore an eye patch and had only three, badly scarred, fingers.

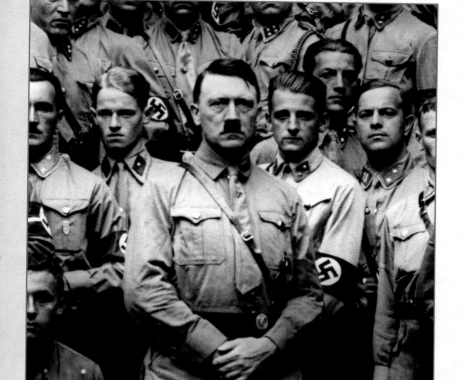

Adolf Hitler (center), Führer of Germany,
started World War II.

PLOTTER

It was while he was recuperating that Claus von Stauffenberg's life took a sudden turn. General Olbricht, head of the General Army Office, appointed Claus his new chief of staff. To choose a seriously wounded man for such an important office may have raised some eyebrows. But Olbricht saw in Claus the two qualities he most wanted in his staff: a love of Germany and a hatred of

Adolf Hitler. Claus von Stauffenberg had stepped into an inner circle of army leaders that included Hans Oster and Henning von Tresckow from the Kreisau Circle. Both had already tried unsuccessfully to assassinate Hitler. Under their guidance, Claus von Stauffenberg became a spy, a plotter, and an assassin.

As the chief of staff under General Olbricht and General Friedrich Fromm, Claus had access to Hitler's schedule and was often present at meetings with the Führer. He and von Tresckow began plotting Operation Valkyrie, often referred to as the "July Plot." The real Operation Valkyrie was an officially approved plan to use the General Army to put down any planned revolts of foreign factory workers. But Claus and his fellow plotters used the term for their own plan. They plotted to kill Hitler, install members of the General Army in his place, and control the Schutzstaffel (SS). The SS was a militant group that served as Hitler's bodyguards and controlled the police and the gathering of intelligence.

The organizers knew killing Hitler would only open the door for other, equally unfit, leaders like Hermann Göring or Heinrich Himmler to take his spot. The conspirators planned to either assassinate them at the same time or immediately after they killed Hitler. They prepared lists of names to take over government positions. Even the announcement of the Führer's death was planned ahead of time. After bungled attempt upon bungled

DID YOU KNOW?

The word "Führer" is a German word for
leader or, as it truly became known,
dictator. The title became associated with
Adolf Hitler when the German president and
supreme commander of the country's armed
forces Paul von Hindenburg died in 1934,
leaving Hitler, then Chancellor of Germany,
as self-proclaimed dictator and Führer.

attempt to get a bomb near Hitler, Claus realized being at Hitler's meetings put him in the best position to carry out the deed and plant a bomb himself.

WOULD-BE ASSASSIN

Carrying a bomb in his briefcase, Claus von Stauffenberg arrived for his July 11, 1944, meeting with Hitler only to be informed by one of his co-conspirators that Göring and Himmler were not present. They decided to wait for a better opportunity.

Their next attempt on July 15 proved no better. Whether it was due to Hitler shortening the meeting or the absence of Himmler, Claus did not detonate his bomb.

Discouraged by the setbacks, the Operation Valkyrie plotters met on July 19 to discuss their next move. Claus had been called

HENNING VON TRESCKOW

Henning von Tresckow, one of the Operation Valkyrie plotters, tried unsuccessfully himself to assassinate Hitler in March 1943. Von Tresckow asked a member of Hitler's staff to carry a package of brandy on board Hitler's plane and deliver it to a friend. Henning rigged the package with a fuse, but it didn't explode. Henning was forced to call the staff member and say he had given him the wrong package by mistake and switch the dud bomb for real bottles of brandy.

to a conference with Hitler scheduled for the next day. Spooked by the failure of their previous attempts, they went over their plan again, determined to succeed this time. After their meeting, Claus visited a church to pray, checked the bombs in his briefcase, and placed a phone call to his wife. However, the phone lines were down and he couldn't reach her.

Claus flew to the conference at Hitler's private hideaway, the Wolf's Lair, the morning of July 20, 1944. He was armed with two bombs in his briefcase. As it was a hot day, Claus asked permission to change his sweat-soaked shirt in a private room. One of his fellow plotters, Werner von Haeften, accompanied him, using the excuse that the one-handed colonel needed assistance changing clothes. Sweat dripping into his eyes, von Stauffenberg used a pair of pliers specially fitted for his three fingers to arm the first bomb.

He was interrupted by a phone call with a reminder the meeting was about to start. Claus knew Hitler didn't tolerate lateness. With only one bomb armed, Claus was out of time. As he walked toward the meeting room, a helpful officer, concerned for the one-handed Colonel von Stauffenberg, tried to help by taking his briefcase. Claus grabbed it back, but turned the man's pity to his advantage, asking that he seat him as close to Hitler as possible due to his hearing loss.

Claus sat three seats down from Hitler. It was 12:35 p.m. in the afternoon. He slid his briefcase under the heavy oak table as close to Hitler as he could reach. Minutes later he asked to be excused to make an urgent phone call. Once he was out of sight, he and von Haeften got in a car. Claus lit a cigarette with trembling fingers. Just as they passed through the security gate at 12:42 p.m., the bomb exploded.

Claus ordered his driver to take them to the airport. Hitler was no doubt dead. The conspirators would declare martial law and, as the heads of the General Army, take over power.

The Wolf's Lair was greatly damaged from the attempt on Hitler's life.

But at 1:30 p.m., one of the conspirators present at Wolf's Lair called General Olbricht. Wary of possible phone bugging, he said, "Something terrible has happened." After pausing he added, "The Führer is alive."

Hitler had scrambled out of the burned, shattered conference room with his hair singed, his right side burned, and his pants shredded. One of the conference attendees had been annoyed by the fact that Claus's briefcase was in his way and moved it farther away from Hitler. Four men died and two were seriously injured in the blast. Had Claus been able to arm both bombs, Hitler would certainly have been among the dead.

Returning to Olbricht's office, Claus heard that Hitler had survived the attack, but he insisted it was a lie. He had seen the explosion himself. They went to urge General Friedrich Fromm—commander of the Nazi regime's reserve forces—to enact martial law. But Fromm refused, asking how he could be certain Hitler was dead. When Claus replied, "I know because I placed the bomb myself," Fromm was horrified. He urged Claus to commit suicide. When he refused, Fromm announced that Claus was under arrest. Instead, the Valkyrie conspirators locked Fromm in an office.

The next few hours were a swirl of confusion as Claus and his fellow conspirators tried to take over the General Army and seize control from Hitler. The plotters called other units and issued orders to arrest Gestapo leaders and seize the communication

Friedrich Fromm stayed loyal to Hitler but was executed in 1945 anyway for failing to foil the assassination plot.

network, but their orders were met with doubt and fear. At 6:30 p.m., German radio stations broadcast an announcement that Adolf Hitler had survived a bomb blast unhurt. The Valkyrie conspirators continued to call members of the General Army, insisting the broadcast was a lie.

That evening a group of armed officers, suspicious of the phone calls and activity, showed up demanding to see General Fromm. The officers freed Fromm, who demanded the conspirators be put to death. Fromm allowed Olbricht to write a letter to his family. General Ludwig Beck requested, and was given, a pistol to commit suicide.

Just after midnight on July 21, 1944, the July Plot reached its resolution. General Friedrich Olbricht, Ritter Mertz von Quirnheim, Werner von Haeften, and Claus von Stauffenberg were lined up outside by the light of a truck's headlights and executed by a makeshift firing squad. Claus von Stauffenberg's last words as he died were, "Long live sacred Germany."

SIPPENHAFT

After the July 20 attack on him, Hitler instituted the practice of *sippenhaft*, or blood-guilt laws, to deter others from committing such crimes. Under sippenhaft, all relatives of someone convicted of a crime, or even suspected of a crime, could be punished or put to death along with the suspected criminal. Claus's wife, Nina, as well as his mother, brothers, uncles, and grandparents were taken to concentration camps. His children were sent to a special children's home for the families of so-called "traitors." Thousands of others, guilty by association with Operation Valkyrie's conspirators, were imprisoned under sippenhaft.

SPIES!

Deep-Cover Spies and Double-Crossers of the

Cold War

COLD WAR
1947 - 1991

The Cold War was a period of time when two superpowers with two different ideologies faced off: the United States, whose ideology was democracy, and the Soviet Union, whose ideology was communism.

In World War II, the Soviet Union and the United States fought together to defeat Germany and Adolf Hitler. However, the United States was uneasy with the dictatorship of Joseph Stalin in the Soviet Union and the principles of communism in general. The Soviet Union was upset and nervous about the United States' advanced technology and atomic weapons, which they'd used against Japan at the end of World War II. Soon after the end of the war the tensions between the two countries overflowed.

In 1947 U.S. president Harry S. Truman announced the Truman Doctrine. He pledged the support—economic, military, and political—of the United States to any nation threatened by authoritarian regimes or forces. This sparked the years of the Cold War where the two superpowers were locked in a struggle over whose ideology would win.

The fight played out in a number of conflicts primarily fought by other nations. Among the many conflicts sparked by this struggle were the civil war in Korea (1950–1953), the long, drawn-out conflict between North and South Vietnam (1955–1975), and the Cuban Missile Crisis (in October of 1962).

Additionally, the United States and the Soviet Union were locked in two other conflicts: the space race and the arms race. The space race was a competition to see which superpower could gain ground in the exploration of space and build the most technologically advanced equipment. When the Soviet Union launched the first satellite, Sputnik, in 1957, the race was on. In 1969, the United States landed on the moon, effectively winning the space race.

One of the most intense aspects of the war, however, was the "arms race." Throughout the Cold War, the Soviet Union and the United States kept escalating the number and scope of the weapons they were stockpiling, including nuclear weapons. The world teetered on the edge of nuclear war. The concept of Mutually Assured Destruction (MAD)—or, the idea that if one country attacked the other with nuclear weapons, the other country would too, ending both countries—seemed to be the only thing keeping the world from total destruction.

Finally, in 1991, the Soviet leader, Mikhail Gorbachev, began dismantling the Soviet Union and its communist economic policies. Countries that had been conquered by the Soviet Union regained their independence and the Soviet Union was dismantled. There are now 15 separate countries that were once part of the Soviet Union.

Both superpowers of the Cold War relied heavily on intelligence gathered by spies. These deep-cover, often double-crossing, operatives played huge roles in the successes and failures of the Cold War. This section explores the lives and deeds of a few of the most influential spies of the Cold War.

Gary Powers flew spy planes over the Soviet Union.

CHAPTER 12

GARY POWERS: THE SPY WHO GOT SWAPPED

Francis Gary Powers should have been suspicious of the job offer right from the start. It began with a mysterious invitation from his commander to apply for another assignment, then a secret evening meeting at a hotel where he was told to ask for Mr. Collins. The offer came with a big salary, more than double what he earned as a pilot for the U.S. Air Force, but Mr. Collins wouldn't tell him exactly what the job was. It was patriotic. It involved travel out of the country. It involved flying.

As Gary Powers soon found out, it also involved a lot of danger. His new employer was the Central Intelligence Agency (CIA). His new job was to fly a just-created secret aircraft called the U-2. The aircraft was a light plane with a fast jet engine that allowed it to fly higher than any other plane and stay in the air for a very long time. The U-2 flew so high that it was nearly invisible and undetectable by radar systems. It was believed that an enemy's surface-to-air missiles (SAMs) couldn't reach it.

The U-2 was the plane Gary Powers used for spying.

Gary was given an alias: Francis G. Palmer. Under this alias, he registered at a Washington D.C. hotel in January 1956 and waited by the phone for instructions from the mysterious Mr. Collins. For the next three months Gary moved from hotel to hotel and room to room for meetings and training sessions. Each time before they spoke, Mr. Collins turned the radio on just in case the room was bugged. During this time the CIA performed lie detector tests as well as rigorous physical and psychological tests on Gary. They had to make sure he could endure the physical strain of flying the U-2 and the emotional stress of not being able to talk about his job.

DID YOU KNOW?

The KGB was the security and
intelligence agency, and secret
police, of the Soviet Union from
1954 to 1991.

TRAINING FOR DUTY

After months of tests and meetings, Gary was sent to a secret training base in the Nevada desert where he learned to fly the U-2. Before he could take to the air, he had to be trained to breathe correctly in high altitudes and engage in hours of "pre-breathing" exercises with pure oxygen. The U-2 was unlike anything he had ever flown before.

The ultra-light plane contained emergency supplies, including a parachute, inflatable life raft, warm clothing, compass, knife, and money from various countries. It also included an item for extreme emergencies: a hollow silver dollar coin containing a suicide pin coated in curare, a lethal poison. It could be used in the event the pilot crashed and was taken into custody in a hostile country.

Gary would be flying over hostile territory indeed. The Soviet Union shot down pilots who wandered into their territory accidentally, and Gary's flights over the USSR would be no accident. The United States had designed the U-2 specifically to fly over the USSR undetected for a job they called Operation Overflight. The plane was equipped with a special camera to take pictures of military bases, missile launch sites, early warning system facilities, and other places the Soviets preferred to keep secret.

Gary Powers spied on the Soviet Union for years with the U-2.

After being transferred overseas, Gary made practice runs from U.S. military bases in Turkey and Pakistan, photographing things along the Soviet border without crossing the boundary. After several months of practicing over friendly territory, Gary was ready for the real mission: penetrating the Soviet border to spy. For the next four years he flew many U-2 flights over the USSR, taking surveillance pictures for both the CIA and the National Security Agency (NSA).

After years of flying the most secret aircraft in the world over hostile territory, the mission had begun to feel routine for Gary. It became a job like any other job. But all that changed in the spring of 1960 during a fateful flight. Gary didn't know it, but it was to be his last U-2 flight. The United States had long underestimated the Soviets' radar technology. But, it was about to become evident that the Soviets could detect the U-2, and that they had been perfecting their surface-to-air missile range. Gary was sent to Peshawar, Pakistan, where the flight would originate, but his flight order was delayed several times over the next few days. The flight was finally authorized and he left Pakistan at 6:26 a.m. on May 1, 1960. His flight would carry him over Russia and end in Norway.

Four hours into the flight, Gary heard a bang as the U-2 shook and an orange flash lit up the sky. Although the missile did not hit the plane directly, the sonic waves resulting from the nearby explosion proved catastrophic. The plane spiraled down. Gary tried to activate the ejection seat, but his legs were trapped. The canopy overhead sailed away. Mirrors snapped off. As bits of the plane broke loose, Gary freed his legs and climbed out. His orange and white parachute ballooned above him and he floated down into enemy territory.

FROM PILOT TO PRISONER

On the way down he had the presence of mind to rip up the maps he was carrying. He also placed the sheathed needle from the silver dollar in his pocket in case he needed it later. He saw a car coming toward him. Upon landing, he was surrounded by villagers. A man emerged from the car and seized his gun. From his bizarre arrival out of the sky and the letters "U.S.A." on the gun handle, they quickly identified Gary as an American pilot. The men placed Gary in the car and drove him to the police station near the Russian city of Sverdlovsk. There Gary watched as a flood of people arrived, each carrying a bit of his destroyed plane.

He was taken into custody and his suicide pin was confiscated. Then he was flown to Moscow for questioning. The questioning continued all day, every day, for 61 days. At night he was locked in a jail cell. He had received no training on what to do in the event of a capture other than directions on using the suicide pin. The only other advice he remembered was, "You might as well tell them everything because they're going to get it out of you anyway." Gary decided to tell the truth when it came to things the Soviets could either easily guess or confirm with the broken U-2 in their possession.

HOLLOW ITEMS

Hollow items like the nickel Rudolf Abel, a Soviet spy, used to hide microfilm and microdots are nothing new. Spies throughout the centuries have hollowed out everyday items and used them to conceal their secrets. Small, dead birds were once cleaned and

He was charged with the state crime of espionage, tried in a Soviet court, and on his 31st birthday, found guilty. Because he cooperated, Francis Gary Powers was given a lenient sentence: 10 years in a Russian prison.

In the Soviet Union, Gary Powers was put on trial for spying.

Taken to Vladimir Prison east of Moscow to serve his term, he was housed with cellmate Zigurd Kruminsh, a Latvian who spoke both Russian and English. Gary's only communication with the outside world came from Soviet radio and newspapers. At first Zigurd translated for him. Later Zigurd taught him enough

Russian so he could understand some of the news himself. Gary was also allowed to receive mail from his wife and parents.

Gary's father, Oliver Powers, not only wrote to his son in jail, he also wrote to another prisoner who he thought might be able to help his son: Colonel Rudolf Abel. Abel, whose real name was Vilyam Fisher, had been incarcerated in a U.S. prison in 1957 for being a Soviet spy. He had transmitted information to the Soviets in various ways, such as by hiding microfilm photos in hollow nickels. Powers wrote to Abel to encourage him to talk Soviet officials into a prisoner exchange, swapping Abel for Gary. James Donovan, Colonel Abel's U.S. defense attorney, thought this was a very good idea.

THE EXCHANGE

On February 7, 1962, a year and nine months into his sentence, Gary Powers returned from a trip to the bathroom to find two KGB officers standing outside his prison cell. The KGB colonel asked Gary if he'd like to go to Moscow the following day. Like the mysterious Mr. Collins, the KGB man would reveal no more. But Gary knew something unusual was up when a guard brought in a small suitcase and told him to pack.

On arriving in Moscow, Gary thought he would be dropped off at the U.S. Embassy. Instead he was informed they were flying to East Germany. On February 10, 1962, the KGB drove Gary

Powers to the Glienicke Bridge, which connected Potsdam, East Germany, to West Berlin in West Germany. At 8:20 a.m. Gary Powers followed five men onto the bridge with armed guards behind him. Across the bridge in the distance he saw another group of men approaching.

Both groups stopped just short of the middle. A man Gary recognized from the U-2 program walked up to him. "What was your high school football coach's name?" he asked. The United States wanted to make sure they weren't getting an imposter before turning Abel over to the KGB. But Gary couldn't, for the life of him, remember the answer he had provided years ago on the forms he had filled out. Had he come this far to be turned back for not remembering the answer to the code question? Thankfully he could provide the names of his wife, his mother, and his dog, which convinced them he was the right person.

Gary waited as the KGB performed a similar interview with Rudolf Abel. When both sides were satisfied, the KGB colonel pushed Francis Gary Powers toward the west side of the bridge. He was free.

DID YOU KNOW?

Another U.S. citizen, Frederic L.
Pryor, was released at Checkpoint
Charlie, a guarded crossing between
East and West Berlin, at the same time
as the exchange of Gary Powers for
Rudolf Abel. Before the Berlin Wall
was built, Pryor conducted university
research in East Berlin. He was held
on suspicion of espionage by the East
Germans, though he was, in fact, merely
a student.

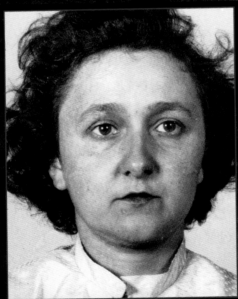

Julius and Ethel Rosenberg sparked much controversy in the
United States and around the world.

CHAPTER 13

JULIUS AND ETHEL ROSENBERG: RED SCARE SPIES

For over 60 years, Julius and Ethel Rosenberg have been known as notorious Soviet spies who lived and worked in the United States. However, the complicated path that ended in their arrest shows a more complex story. What became of the Rosenbergs to this day remains controversial.

It all started with a KGB codebook found in Finland during World War II. The codebook eventually allowed the Federal Bureau of Investigation (FBI) to read communications intercepted from the Soviet Union. One document they deciphered was a report on the Manhattan Project by German-born British physicist Klaus Fuchs. Fuchs was one of the principal scientists who worked on the atomic bomb for the United States.

When the British Security Service confronted Fuchs in early 1950 with the codebook evidence of his treachery, he confessed. He admitted to spilling U.S. and British atomic secrets to the Soviets. Under questioning, Fuchs said he passed his information along to a handler known as Raymond. After some investigation, the FBI discovered that Raymond was really Harry Gold, a U.S. citizen who worked as a chemist. Gold had become a spy for the Soviet Union. The FBI arrested Gold and grilled him for the names of his other contacts. He confessed and mentioned an arranged meeting with a soldier stationed at Los Alamos who lived in Albuquerque, New Mexico. Gold couldn't remember the soldier's name but described his appearance, the neighborhood he lived in, and his wife's name.

A FAMILY OF SPIES

From Gold's information, the FBI identified the soldier as David Greenglass. Greenglass had worked as an assistant foreman in the atomic bomb high explosives unit in Los Alamos. When questioned, Greenglass admitted passing secret atomic information to Harry Gold.

David Greenglass wasn't finished, though: he named his own family members, the Rosenbergs, as spies as well. Greenglass said that Julius Rosenberg—married to David's sister, Ethel—had set up the meeting with Gold. According to Greenglass (though his claims varied), he and his wife, Ruth, dined at the Rosenbergs' New York apartment one night during Greenglass' military leave. Greenglass claimed that during that dinner, Julius Rosenberg talked him into writing down everything he knew about Los Alamos and the atomic bomb.

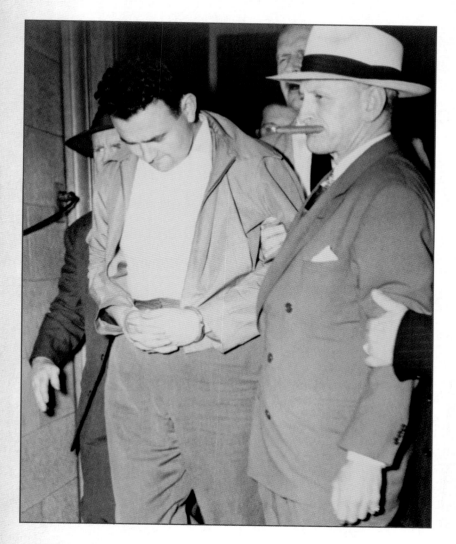

David Greenglass was arrested for spying and soon pointed to Julius and Ethel Rosenberg as fellow spies.

Also according to David Greenglass, Julius said he would arrange for a courier—Harry Gold—to pick up Greenglass' notes when he returned home to New Mexico. Since neither David Greenglass nor his wife had ever met Harry Gold, Julius came up with a way for the Greenglasses to recognize the unknown courier. Julius tore the front label off a box of gelatin and cut it into two puzzle pieces. He gave one puzzle piece to the Greenglasses. Later, Harry Gold arrived in Albuquerque and showed the other half of the gelatin label to the Greenglasses. David Greenglass gave him the notes on Los Alamos and the atomic bomb. In return, Harry Gold gave David Greenglass $500.

David and his wife, Ruth, along with Ethel and Julius Rosenberg, had all been members of the Communist Party years earlier. Even during the Red Scare, the Rosenbergs held Communist Party meetings at their home and encouraged their friends and neighbors to attend. According to David Greenglass, Julius began spying for the Soviet Union.

Greenglass reported that while Julius was employed in the Signal Corps he stole fuses and other small weaponry parts as well as instruction manuals. He served as a courier, picking up drops at a movie theater and delivering items to a Soviet agent. Greenglass claimed Julius rented a secret apartment from which he ran his spy ring and photographed secret documents. As Julius became more involved with the party, he and Ethel canceled their subscriptions to communist newspapers and dropped their party memberships so as to not arouse any suspicion.

On July 17, 1950, as the Rosenbergs' older son sat listening to *The Lone Ranger* on the radio, the FBI arrested Julius Rosenberg in

DID YOU KNOW?

Many years later David Greenglass
changed his story, saying that his
wife, Ruth, had done the typing, so
he had implicated Ethel to save Ruth.
Afterward he claimed he couldn't
remember who had done what.

his apartment. He was charged with recruiting David Greenglass into espionage in 1944. Unlike the others arrested, Julius Rosenberg did not confess and refused to name his conspirators.

David Greenglass also implicated his sister, Ethel Rosenberg, in the spy ring, insisting she had typed some of the documents passed to Harry Gold.

Evidence against Ethel was weak, but in an effort to pressure Julius to talk, Ethel was arrested on August 11, 1950, following a grand jury investigation. She was not even allowed to make child-care arrangements for her and Julius' two sons, Michael and Robert.

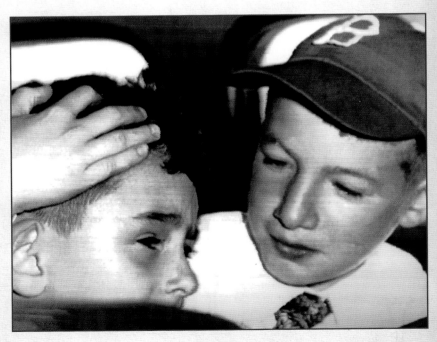

The Rosenberg children comfort each other during their parents' trial.

THE TRIAL OF THE CENTURY

On March 6, 1951, the Rosenberg trial began. They were charged with conspiracy to commit espionage, a charge that could result in the death penalty. Both Julius and Ethel proclaimed their innocence. They refused to answer some of the questions posed to them, citing their Fifth Amendment right (the right to not be witnesses against themselves). During jury deliberations a lone juror at first held out against conviction because his conscience couldn't bear the idea of a mother of two young boys being executed. By the next morning that juror yielded and the Rosenbergs were found guilty.

RED SCARE

Following World War II, as the Soviet Union's power and influence grew, an anti-communist attitude and widespread fear of Soviet espionage spread across the United States. Fueled by hearings of the House Un-American Activities Committee, many Americans faced accusations of being communists or affiliating with communists. In Hollywood entertainers suspected of being "reds" (so-called because the Soviet Union's flag was red) were blacklisted and couldn't find work. Many union leaders, college professors, government employees, those suspected of being gay, and numerous other groups of people were hauled before the House Un-American Activities Committee and questioned about their loyalty to the United States. Senator Joseph McCarthy added fuel to the fire by claiming to have a list of spies who were members of the Communist Party, though in actuality, there was no such list.

Before sentencing Julius and Ethel Rosenberg to death, Judge Irving Kaufman said:

"I believe your conduct in putting into the hands of the Russians the A-bomb years before our best scientists predicted Russia would perfect the bomb has already caused, in my opinion, the Communist aggression in Korea, with the resultant casualties exceeding fifty thousand and who knows but that millions more of innocent people may pay the price of your treason."

The Rosenbergs were the only defendants in the atomic spy trials to receive the death penalty, because they alone refused to name others. In exchange for testifying against the Rosenbergs, David Greenglass was sentenced to only 15 years in prison. In separate trials, Harry Gold was given 30 years, and Klaus Fuchs received 14 years. All of them later had their sentences greatly reduced.

For more than two years the Rosenbergs appealed their case. The appeal went all the way to the Supreme Court. On June 14, 1953, their 10-year-old son, Michael Rosenberg, delivered a handwritten letter to a guard at the White House. In it he begged President Eisenhower to grant his mommy and daddy clemency.

The court granted a temporary stay of execution on June 17, 1953. In response to the stay, more than 21,000 telegrams flooded into the White House asking for clemency. Thousands

> Dear Mr. President,
>   Please don't leave my brother and I without a Mommy and Daddy.
>   They have always been good to us. We love them very much.
>   Michael and Robert Rosenberg
>   36 Laurel Hill Terrace
>   New York, N.Y.

The Rosenbergs' son Michael wrote a letter to President Eisenhower.

of protesters picketed around the White House, demanding the execution be permanently overturned.

The following day was the Rosenbergs' 14th wedding anniversary. They spent the day writing letters and drafting their wills. The final decision on whether they would live or die was about to be handed down. In preparation, newspapers even had two different headlines standing by: "Rosenbergs Executed" and "Rosenbergs Saved." But there was to be no salvation for the Rosenbergs. On June 19, 1953, the Supreme Court reversed the stay, allowing the execution to go forward.

The executions were set for 11:00 p.m. on Friday, June 19, 1953. Hoping for an extension, the Rosenbergs' lawyer argued that a death sentence after sundown on a Friday desecrated the Jewish Sabbath. In response the warden moved the execution time up to 8:00 p.m. Julius and Ethel were allowed to spend their last afternoon of life together with a wire mesh wall separating them. They wrote a letter to their children. With their execution time moved up, they did not eat a last meal. At 7:20 p.m. they were separated.

ROBERT AND MICHAEL MEEROPOL

After Julius and Ethel Rosenberg were executed, their sons, Robert and Michael, were adopted by Anne and Abel Meeropol. For decades, the Rosenberg brothers (now Meeropol brothers) fought to prove their parents, Julius and Ethel, were innocent. After a convicted Cold War spy released a statement in 2008, however, the brothers now believe their father was a Soviet spy. What he gave to the Soviets, though, did not amount to stealing atomic secrets, they say. The brothers also maintain that their mother, Ethel, was

Before following her husband to the electric chair in New York's Sing Sing Prison, Ethel wrote a final letter to her lawyer, Manny Bloch, ending with the words, "We are the first victims of American Fascism."

DAILY NEWS
NEW YORK'S PICTURE NEWSPAPER

FINAL ★★★★

Vol. 34. No. 309   New York 17, N.Y., Saturday, June 20, 1953•   4¢

SPIES DIE IN CHAIR

By HENRY LEE

Julius and Ethel Rosenberg, the A-traitors who for two years had tried to out-bluff Uncle Sam with the help of fellow Communists all over the world, finally were executed at Sing Sing Prison shortly after 8 o'clock last night.

The mousy Julius, his mustache shaved off, entered the death chamber first, at 8:04 P. M. and was pronounced dead, after the customary three electric shocks, at 8:06¾.

But when Ethel followed at 8:11½ P. M., it required five shocks to complete the death sentence, and she was not pronounced dead till 8:16 P. M. She had already been unstrapped when Drs. H. W. Kipp and George McCracken

ordered the executioner to give her two more shocks.

Both died calmly—and silently. There had been some speculation that, near the end, they might crack and take advantage of government offers to save their lives by making a clean breast of their spy operation. There had been some belief, too, that they might die chanting the dreary Communist slogans by which they had lived. But they fooled everybody—and their fellow Commies fooled them. Not one showed up in Ossining to carry on the demonstrations which the Commies have been staging all over the world for the

[Continued on page 3, col. 1]

Newspapers followed the Rosenbergs' case closely.

George Blake became one of the most notorious double agents of the Cold War.

CHAPTER 14

GEORGE BLAKE: JAILBIRD SPY

George Behar was born into a multicultural Dutch family: one that loved all things British. His Turkish father, Albert, married a Dutch woman and settled in the Netherlands. Albert became a naturalized British citizen and proudly named his son after the British king, George VI. He even changed his family's last name to Blake to make it sound more English. So, perhaps it was fortunate that Albert didn't live to see his scandalous son's name splashed across British newspaper headlines.

Following his father's death, George was sent to Cairo to live with relatives. His mother hoped he would have better educational opportunities in Egypt. There he learned French and English, in addition to his native Dutch.

Despite living in Egypt, he visited his family in the Netherlands whenever he could. It was during one such visit to his grandmother in May 1940 that the Germans invaded the Netherlands. His mother and sister, in another town, escaped to Britain, thinking he would soon follow.

Because he was a British citizen and the British were at

war with the Germans, George was taken into custody by the Germans and interned in a prisoner-of-war camp. But since he was only 16 years old, they soon released him. He wasn't old enough to be considered a threat. His prison experience, along with the invasion of the Netherlands, made George Blake angry enough to fight back. He joined the Dutch Resistance and carried secret packages and information across the country. With help from the Resistance, he plotted his escape to Britain to join his mother and sister. Along his escape route he traveled the Dutch countryside and stayed at safe houses. He was smuggled across the border to Spain, only to be imprisoned again, this time by Spanish authorities. Though Spain was officially neutral during the war, they collaborated with Nazi Germany and guarded their borders against those trying to escape German occupation.

ADVENTURE AND SECRETS

After holding George in captivity for months, Spanish authorities located his mother and he was finally released to travel to Britain. Upon arriving, George Blake volunteered to serve in the Royal Navy. After completing his training he applied to work in Special Services because he liked the idea of adventure and secrets. Once he passed the interviews and language tests, his knowledge of the Dutch Resistance landed George an assignment with the Dutch section of the British Secret Intelligence Service.

After World War II ended, the British Secret Intelligence Service sent George to language school to learn a fourth language: Russian. Following the completion of his course, George expected to be placed in an Eastern Bloc country, controlled by the Soviet Union, to use his new language skills. Instead, he was surprised when he was placed in South Korea in 1948. It was an event that would alter the course of his life.

Shortly after George arrived, North Korea crossed the 38th parallel and invaded South Korea on June 25, 1950. Within days, George Blake was captured and put in a prisoner-of-war camp because he was a British citizen. While imprisoned for a year and a half, George became convinced the communist ideology was correct. He turned against his adopted homeland. One day he handed his Korean guard a note written in Russian and addressed to the Soviet Embassy, asking for a meeting.

At the meeting, George Blake offered to betray Britain and work as a double agent for the Soviets. The Soviets could hardly refuse his offer. After all, he was already a spy who spoke fluent Russian. He refused to accept any payment for his services, stating later, "I did what I did for ideological reasons, never for money." When he was released from prison with other POWs and returned to Britain, the first thing he did was meet with the British Secret Intelligence Service to resume his intelligence work. A few weeks later, he traveled to the Netherlands and met with his new KGB handler. He was given a small Minox camera to photograph British documents. He worked overtime to comb through classified files for information his Soviet handler could use. Every three to four weeks he met his contact near a London subway station to deliver information. During their clandestine meetings, George Blake revealed the names of other British spies to the KGB as well as any KGB double agents working for the British. In doing so, he doomed many of his fellow spies to death.

When George was reassigned to West Berlin, he was able to bring with him a stunning piece of intelligence for his Soviet friends in East Berlin. The British, along with the Americans, were building a tunnel to conceal phone-tapping equipment. The equipment would allow them to eavesdrop on communications at the Soviet Army headquarters. For years, the British thought their tunnel was a rousing success. Finally, the Soviets "discovered" the tap in 1956 and the operation was shut down. The KGB had known about the tap all along thanks to their double agent.

George Blake was one of the most successful double spies ever, but in 1960 George's own game caught up to him. The spy who had double-crossed dozens of his fellow spies was caught when a Polish spy defected to the United States and named George Blake as a double agent. George was called back to Britain and questioned for several days. He finally cracked when he was asked if he had defected under the duress of torture during his

DID YOU KNOW?

Following World War II, Germany was divided into two sections. West Germany was occupied by Britain, the United States, and France. It was run as a capitalist state. East Germany was occupied by the Soviet Union and run as a socialist state. A wall in Berlin with guarded checkpoints divided West Berlin from East Germany from 1961 to 1989.

Korean imprisonment. He yelled, "No, nobody tortured me! No, nobody blackmailed me! I myself approached the Soviets and offered my services . . ."

SORRY? NOT SORRY

George was arrested. During the sentencing at his trial his lawyer wanted to say that George was "deeply sorry for all he had done," but George refused to allow it, saying it was untrue. He felt what he had done was right. The British court sentenced him to

WIRETAPPING

In George Blake's day, all phones were hardwired into buildings. To "tap" them, an electrical wire had to be installed to allow a person or people to listen in on conversations. If the wires were found, the victim knew his phone had been tapped. Today it's even easier to tap into both landline and cell phones. No wires need to be installed. Digital signals just have to be diverted so a third party can listen in. This makes it almost impossible for victims to know their phones have been tapped.

Wiretapping is still a spy technique used today.

42 years in jail. The newspapers had a field day, claiming, in error, George Blake received one year for every British spy he betrayed.

Imprisoned for the fourth time in his life, George Blake decided he would not stay for long. He befriended fellow inmate Sean Bourke. When Sean was released, the two hatched George's escape plan. Sean created a rope ladder with knitting needle rungs, which he slung over the prison wall. While most of the guards and prisoners were attending a movie, George Blake climbed over the wall and into Sean's waiting car. Another friend hid him in a secret compartment of a van. They traveled all the way to the East Berlin checkpoint, and from there the Soviets transported Blake to the Soviet Union.

George Blake was welcomed into Soviet life with an elegantly furnished house, a personal housekeeper and chauffeur, and a lifetime pension for his services. In his new comfortable life, he took a job in Soviet publishing and later wrote a book for a British publisher about his life as a double-crossing spy. It became a best-seller. But, the joke turned out to be on him. After only receiving one payment, the British courts stepped in and stopped him from receiving any further money from book sales, ruling he could not profit from his crimes. So, the double-crossing spy got double-crossed in the end.

Janet Chisholm became an important spy for the British government.

CHAPTER 15

JANET CHISHOLM: THE BABY BUGGY SPY

Janet Anne Deane Chisholm never intended to be a spy. But her life changed when she married one. She met her spy husband while she was working as a secretary in the British Intelligence Office. Her husband, Ruari Chisholm, became the British MI6 head of a station in Moscow. MI6 gathered intelligence from foreign countries. Officially his job title was embassy visa officer, but it was merely a cover for his intelligence work.

The posting to the Soviet Union was a welcome one to Janet, even though the British Secret Intelligence Service considered living in Moscow a hardship. She was no stranger to living in locations outside of Britain. Her father had been a British Royal Engineer and she was born at the foot of the Himalaya Mountains in the British Indies in 1929. She already knew Russian because she'd learned it at boarding school in England. All in all, Janet was well prepared for life in Moscow and the unexpected spy adventure that awaited her there.

Janet Chisholm felt at home in Russia.

Quick-thinking and levelheaded, Janet was the perfect "cut-out," or go-between, for her husband when Russian Colonel Oleg Penkovsky decided to turn against the Soviet Union. Penkovsky felt that Soviet leader Nikita Khrushchev's aggressive stockpiling of weapons would lead to another world war. However, Penkovsky couldn't risk being seen with a known employee of the British Embassy like Ruari, so Janet took his place. She would be the contact who would do "live-drop" deliveries from Penkovsky.

Janet's first meeting with Oleg Penkovsky was arranged by traveling businessman and British spy Grenville Wynne. Wynne met Penkovsky and gave him a Minox camera and film to photograph documents. He showed Penkovsky a picture of Janet Chisholm, code-named Anne, and directed him to meet Janet at a Moscow park on Tsvetnoy Boulevard on a prearranged date.

AN AFTERNOON AT THE PARK

On Sunday, July 2, 1961, Janet brought her three small children to the park for some summer sun. When they sat down on a bench, Penkovsky approached and chatted with Janet and the children like a grandfatherly man. He patted one of her blond children on the head and offered the child a box of Russian chocolates. The box contained seven rolls of undeveloped Minox film and photocopies of Soviet missile reports. Janet thanked him for his kindness to the children and put Penkovsky's box in her baby buggy. She covered the fake chocolates with a blanket and pulled an identical box of real chocolates from the buggy, which she offered to her children. This was the first of many exchanges the two made.

While a couple of strolls in the park with candy wouldn't arouse the KGB's suspicions, too many certainly would, so Janet and Penkovsky had to vary their routine. After her ballet class, Janet sometimes stopped in a secondhand store to browse through the used china and crystal. Penkovsky, code-named Hero, would enter, wait for her to notice him, then leave the store. Janet followed him at a distance until he entered an apartment building stairwell or alley for their brief meetings. If anyone walked by when they were together, Penkovsky and Janet embraced and acted like lovers as he slipped cigarette packages containing photo film and documents into Janet's shopping bag.

After one of their hand-off meetings, Penkovsky noticed a suspicious car making a U-turn on a one-way street. Two men in dark overcoats were following Janet in a car. Penkovsky became nervous, fearing Janet had been made, or identified, as a spy. He suggested they change their operation from clandestine meetings to social meetings at embassy cocktail parties. Cocktail parties were common events in which embassy employees and their families mingled with local dignitaries like Penkovsky, so he thought their casual social interactions wouldn't arouse suspicion.

PARTIES ARE TIRING

At one party, Janet, then seven months pregnant, was "introduced" to Colonel Penkovsky by the host. Penkovsky said, "You must be feeling tired. Why don't you rest for a few minutes in the hostess' bedroom?" Janet asked the hostess to lie down, blaming her tiredness on her pregnancy. A few minutes later Penkovsky asked the hostess to show him her lovely home. When they came to the bedroom and found Janet lying down, Penkovsky walked up to the bed, apologized for disturbing her, turned around, and flashed a cigarette package filled with information behind his back. Janet took it without the hostess ever being the wiser.

Janet gave the missile reports and film concealed inside the cigarette packages and candy boxes to her husband, Ruari. They never spoke of the operation out loud in their home in case the house was bugged. Ruari brought the information to the

LIVE-DROPS, BRUSH PASSES, AND DEAD DROPS

A live-drop is when a spy hands documents or goods to his or her handler in an inconspicuous way, while acknowledging each other. Janet Chisholm and Oleg Penkovsky used empty chocolate boxes and cigarette packages in their live-drops. When an item is given without any acknowledgment it's called a brush pass. For example, walking past someone and slipping something into the other's coat pocket is a brush pass. When a spy leaves something for someone, such as an item inside a newspaper left on a park bench, this is called a dead drop.

Colonel Oleg Penkovsky helped the British gather much
information from the KGB.

British Embassy and sent it to Britain in diplomatic pouches.

Those in the embassy developed the film, studied the documents,

and shared some of the information with the U.S. CIA.

Although she and Penkovsky were no longer meeting in

public, Janet continued to visit the park with her children and to

stop in the secondhand shop. She wanted to make it appear as

though these things were part of her regular routine in case the

KGB was watching her as Penkovsky suspected. As it turned out,

Penkovsky had good reason to be suspicious. Ruari and Janet

Chisholm had served in West Berlin at the same time as George

Blake, whom they knew. Blake had reported Ruari as a spy to the KGB, and they had been watching the Chisholm family since the day they moved to Moscow.

After photographing Janet Chisholm walking into a strange apartment building just after one of their own colonels, the KGB had figured out Penkovsky was passing intelligence to the British. But the KGB didn't pounce on Penkovsky right away. Instead, they followed him and watched to see if he might lead them to other spies. When the KGB was satisfied that Penkovsky was only meeting with Janet, they made their move. Colonel Oleg Penkovsky was quietly arrested on October 22, 1962. Penkovsky was accused of treason and tried before the same judge who had found American U-2 pilot Gary Powers guilty. On May 11, 1963, Oleg Penkovsky was found guilty and sentenced to die. The court also pronounced Ruari and Janet Chisholm *personae non gratae*, or unwelcome people, and expelled them from the Soviet Union. As diplomats, they could not be tried for any crimes.

At the time of Oleg Penkovsky's arrest, U.S. president John F. Kennedy and Soviet leader Nikita Krushchev were embroiled in the Cuban Missile Crisis. For 13 days in October 1962, they were in a heated standoff over the Soviets' accumulation of nuclear-capable missiles in Cuba. Both sides feared the other would cast the first weapon in a global nuclear war. But President Kennedy

The Cuban Missile Crisis was one of the most intense conflicts in world history.

had an advantage over Krushchev. He had seen Oleg Penkovsky's pictures and reports and knew Krushchev didn't have the missile strength or range that he claimed. This information allowed Kennedy to hold out until Krushchev offered to remove the Cuban missiles if the Americans would agree not to invade Cuba.

A worldwide nuclear disaster was averted thanks in part to a Russian colonel with a chocolate box and a woman with a baby buggy.

DID YOU KNOW?

In 1962 the Soviets stockpiled nuclear
missiles that could reach the United
States from the Soviet's ally state, Cuba.
President John F. Kennedy placed a naval
blockade around Cuba in October of 1962 to
prevent any further missile shipments from
arriving. Tensions between the two countries
increased, but a nuclear war was averted
when they reached an agreement whereby the
Soviet Union removed missiles from Cuba and
the United States agreed not to invade Cuba.

Pham Xuan An was beloved by those on both sides of the
Vietnam conflict.

CHAPTER 16

PHAM XUAN AN: VIETNAM'S REPORTER SPY

Part of Pham Xuan An's name means "secret" in Vietnamese. This is fitting because he kept many secrets in his life, starting in the late 1940s in Vietnam. During that time period, Vietnam was part of a French colony known as French Indochina. Pham Xuan An organized student protests against the French occupiers and the Americans in Saigon. As an ardent nationalist, Pham Xuan An wanted an independent Vietnam free of outside control. He thought the Communist Party would bring this about, so he joined the movement. One day the Viet Minh, members of a group dedicated to Vietnamese independence and the advancement of communism, asked to meet with him. Pham Xuan An was told he had been selected for a more important role than student organizer. The Viet Minh planned to train him as an intelligence officer.

Pham Xuan An was an ideal spy candidate against the Americans because he had learned some English from

Many troops fought for a socialist Vietnam.

missionaries in his youth. From then on, whenever he met an English speaker, he asked that person to help him study English. People were happy to help the friendly, hardworking young man. As a cover for his real work, the Viet Minh directed Pham Xuan An to study journalism and learn more about American customs.

IT HELPS TO HAVE FRIENDS

In an odd twist of fate, the people who arranged Pham Xuan An's travel and college tuition in the United States were both involved in the CIA and working against the Viet Minh to stop the spread of communism. Pham Xuan An met one of these men, Colonel Edward Lansdale, while working as a Vietnamese translator for him. Lansdale took an immediate liking to An and offered to send him to intelligence school to train as a CIA spy.

As An was already involved in intelligence for the other side, he instead asked him for help in becoming a journalist. Through Lansdale's contacts at the Asia Foundation, arrangements were made for An to study in the United States. Another of Pham Xuan An's friends, Mills Brandes, who unbeknownst to An was a CIA operative, gave him names of family and friends in the United States to contact once he arrived there.

So, with the unwitting help of the CIA, the Viet Minh's secret spy, Pham Xuan An, arrived in sunny California on October 12, 1957, to study journalism at Orange Coast College in Costa Mesa. Pham Xuan An loved journalism and loved life in the United States even more. He wrote for the student newspaper, lived in the dorms, enjoyed dances and luaus, visited Disneyland, and bought a used car. He made many friends and was very popular. After a summer internship at the *Sacramento Bee* newspaper, Pham Xuan An drove across the country for a second internship at the United

Nations. After turning down a job offer to teach Vietnamese at the Department of Defense language school in Monterey, California, Pham Xuan An returned to his homeland to begin his cover identity as a journalist.

In Vietnam he got a job as an assistant with the news agency Reuters, serving as a translator and explaining Vietnamese politics and culture. He also worked for the *Vietnam Press* as a reporter and journalism teacher for other spies to help them establish cover identities as reporters. But Pham Xuan An took journalism almost as seriously as he did spying. He complained that the spies he taught didn't take their journalism classes seriously and would quickly be discovered.

VIETNAM WAR

The Vietnam War (also known as the Second Indochina War) was waged from November 1, 1955, to April 30, 1975. The country of Vietnam was divided into North Vietnam, known as the Democratic Republic of Vietnam, and South Vietnam. The North was supported by the Soviet Union, China, and other communist countries. The South was backed by the United States, South Korea, Australia, and other countries wanting to fend off the advancement of communism. Americans refer to the events of April 30, 1975, as "The Fall of Saigon," while some Vietnamese, especially in the North, refer to it as "Reunification Day."

Pham Xuan An was so good at journalism he later worked for *Time* magazine in Vietnam, covering the war as a full correspondent rather than a local assistant. He knew everyone in politics and the military. His predictions of North Vietnamese tactics were always spot-on, much to the astonishment of other *Time* reporters. Some of his colleagues felt certain he worked for the CIA because his information was always so good. Of course, it helped that he knew exactly what the North Vietnamese planned because he was secretly one of their colonels.

Pham Xuan An often disappeared from his journalism job for days at a time. He explained his absences by also working as a dog trainer, saying he had to work at his other job. If anyone questioned him further he'd hint at visiting a secret lover. In reality, he did have to work at his other job, traveling to meet with the Vietcong, checking drop sites for messages, and processing reports of American troop movements he gathered as a journalist.

EGG ROLLS, SPY-STYLE

He relayed messages in more clandestine ways as well. After photographing sensitive documents for the Vietcong, he rolled the undeveloped film in egg roll wrappers, then tied the egg rolls together with brown paper on which he had written in invisible ink. He took his dogs out for a stroll in the local open-air market stalls and met his contact. The two chatted about the goods on

DID YOU KNOW?

Pham Xuan An made invisible ink himself.
He placed a few grains of rice and a bit
of water in a spoon. Then he heated the
spoon over a fire until the rice turned into
liquid. He then dipped a dry pen into it
and used the liquid rice to write invisible
messages. When his wrapping paper messages
were received, another agent would brush an
iodine mixture over the paper to view the
secret message.

display. Pham Xuan An produced the egg rolls, pretending he had bought them at the open-air market, and offered them to his contact. She would then take them and hand them over to the military.

As the Vietnam War progressed, the North grew stronger and it became apparent the Vietcong would soon take over Saigon in South Vietnam. Journalists scrambled to get out of the country. *Time* magazine offered to fly Pham Xuan An and his family out of Vietnam. Although a man in An's position as a colonel had little to fear from the North's advance, he sent his wife and children to the United States aboard a CBS News airplane, fearing a door-to-door gun battle. Pham Xuan An himself stayed behind, claiming he needed to take care of his aging mother. He brought her to a room abandoned by one of his fleeing colleagues at the Continental Hotel to await the arrival of his fellow North Vietnamese.

It didn't take long for them to arrive. On April 29, 1975, Armed Forces radio in Saigon played Bing Crosby's song "White Christmas" over and over. It was the signal that all U.S. personnel must evacuate immediately.

Although Pham Xuan An supported the Vietcong, he was extremely loyal to his American friends. When An realized one of them still hadn't left, he rushed him to the American Embassy and pushed him under the gate so his friend could evacuate from one of

When the North Vietnamese captured Saigon,
many Americans had to flee.

the last rooftop helicopters before Saigon was completely taken over by the North Vietnamese.

The following day, April 30, 1975, An was the lone employee of *Time* magazine in Vietnam. He sent a message stating, "All American correspondents evacuated. . . . *Time* is now manned by

Pham Xuan An." Within 24 hours the North Vietnamese took over South Vietnam and hoisted their flag over Saigon.

Nearly two decades later, Pham Xuan An's son An Pham wanted to study journalism just like his father had done in the United States. By then Pham Xuan An's spying had long been revealed. Although his former colleagues knew of his deceit, they held him in high esteem as a journalist. So, they banded together to arrange for his son to study journalism at the University of North Carolina at Chapel Hill. Later, when Pham Xuan An died, many of the journalists he once worked with traveled to Vietnam to attend his funeral. They came to pay their last respects to a man they considered their colleague.

Cyber Spies and Secret Agents of Modern Times

In the age of social media and globalization, being a spy comes with a new set of challenges. In World War I, World War II, and the Cold War, spies had a specific nation or group of nations they worked against to win a war. As the world moved more into the digital age, the scope of spying became much broader. Today, enemies can be countries, terrorist groups, leagues of nations, or even individuals acting alone.

On September 11, 2001, the United States suffered one of the worst terrorist attacks the country had ever seen. The terrorist group, al-Qaida, consisted of a relatively small band of religious extremists bent on the destruction of the United States. Their successful terrorist attack spurred the United States and other countries around the world to develop new spying techniques, new cutting-edge equipment, and new, knowledgeable recruits to meet the challenge of 21st century enemies and threats.

In this section, you'll meet a few spies who have been exposed or caught, but most of today's spies still hide in the shadows, working against their enemies. So, here you'll get a glimpse of the new world of cyber spies and secret agents, and will learn along the way that anyone could be a spy next door. Even better, you might just learn that you have the skills of a modern-day spy—how will you use your new-found talents?

Terrorists attacked the World Trade Center in New York City on September 11, 2001.

CHAPTER 17

GAME CHANGER: HOW SEPTEMBER 11 CHANGED THE SPY WORLD

The last thing the Catholic priest, Father Jean-Marie Benjamin, expected was to become a spy. He didn't know that in early September 2001, in Todi, Italy, he would do just that. The day began as a joyful one—he married a young couple and was enjoying their wedding reception. During the celebration, one of the guests sidled up to him. The man whispered to Father Benjamin that something terrible was about to happen. An Islamist terrorist group was planning a deadly attack on the United States. They were going to hijack passenger planes and use them as suicide weapons.

Why would anyone give an Italian priest this information? Father Benjamin happened to be an expert on Islamic culture. Before he became a priest he had worked for the United Nations. For years he had worked with various Islamic charities in Iraq. The question was what would he do with that information? Would he shrug it off as too incredible to be true? Or would he take it seriously?

Father Benjamin suspected the terrorist threat was real. In the days after the wedding, he went to several Italian politicians and a judge with this explosive news, begging them to take action. They were as alarmed as he was. But the wedding guest had not known when or exactly where the attacks would take place.

It turned out that Father Benjamin wasn't the only person who knew something was coming. Spies from around the world had been warned too. The moment that the anonymous wedding guest shared that information with Father Benjamin, the priest unwittingly became part of a mysterious new international network. The network included spies from around the world who had a dangerous secret: they'd heard that there would be an attack on the United States.

SPIES AROUND THE WORLD GET EARLY WARNINGS

The first clue that something was happening came in 1999—two years before the attack. British spies sent a secret report to the United States. The report said that the Islamist extremist group al-Qaida was planning some kind of terrorist attack with airplanes. In the months leading up to 9/11, other spies around the world began hearing disturbing intelligence of a big attack that was being planned. In June, German agents warned the United States, Israel, and Great Britain of a plan that Middle Eastern terrorist

DID YOU KNOW?

Al-Qaida is an international terrorist
group, founded by Osama bin Laden and
other radical Islamists. Bin Laden
formed the group in the 1980s when
Afghanistan was at war with the Soviet
Union. After the war, al-Qaida became
a terrorist force fighting against all
governments that it believed to be anti-
Islamist, including the United States.

Osama Bin Laden was the mastermind behind
the 9/11 attacks.

groups would use hijacked planes as bombs. In July, an Egyptian secret agent undercover in Afghanistan, reported that 20 al-Qaida members were in the United States training to fly small airplanes. Egyptian intelligence passed the information to the United States, but no one acted on the information.

Warnings continued to trickle in from around the world. A Moroccan undercover agent who had joined al-Qaida sent a message to the United States saying bin Laden was planning a huge attack in the fall. Intelligence agents in the country of Jordan intercepted a secret message that said a big attack on the United States was coming. According to the message, terrorists would use airplanes to attack somewhere inside the United States. The agent even knew the secret code name for the attack: Big Wedding.

Russian agents began hearing intel of an attack, too. According to the Russian spies, terrorists were training to fly suicide missions into U.S. targets. Those warnings also went straight to U.S. intelligence agencies. In August 2001, only a few weeks before Father Benjamin got his news, British agents sent two more warnings of al-Qaida hijackings in the United States to then-Prime Minister Tony Blair.

Some U.S. agents took the threats seriously. On August 6, 2001, Central Intelligence Agency (CIA) operatives gave President George W. Bush a paper titled, "Bin Laden Determined to Strike in U.S." But no actions were taken.

AN INTELLIGENCE DISASTER

On September 11, 2001, all the international warnings came terribly true. Al-Qaida operatives who had been living undercover in the United States hijacked four commercial U.S. airplanes. Their leader, Osama bin Laden, had given them their suicide mission: to attack and destroy the World Trade Center in New York City and the Pentagon and the White House in Washington, D.C. Three hijacked planes hit their targets and one crashed in a Pennsylvania field.

How could a well-known international terrorist group launch the biggest surprise attack on the United States since World War II? Especially since the United States had so many warnings from spies around the world. The 9/11 attacks turned out to be an enormous U.S. intelligence failure.

Why didn't anyone listen to the warnings from international spies? U.S. intelligence agencies didn't really believe the threat. They didn't have operatives in the field to confirm all the warnings. Instead, they had to rely on international spies, and those spies didn't have specifics, such as what day the attack was to happen, or what city was the target. The information from around the world was never put together in one place in the United States, so no specific agency had the full picture of what bin Laden was planning. Some agents had some pieces of information, while others got different intel. This failure to communicate allowed the attackers to take the United States by surprise.

The United States Pentagon, which houses the U.S. Department of Defense, was one of the targets in the 9/11 attacks.

Actual U.S. spies were also in short supply. In the 1990s, the CIA and other intelligence organizations weren't sure who to spy on any more. The Cold War with the former Soviet Union—now broken up into Russia and several other countries—was over. The United States no longer had any traditional enemies. The CIA and other agencies recruited fewer agents and started relying more on computers and cyber spying. Slowly, many of the vital human connections with international agents disappeared. New agents were too busy monitoring Internet threats to cultivate important human allies and contacts around the world. After 9/11, U.S. intelligence organizations realized that had been a big mistake.

A NEW WORLD OF SECRETS AND SPIES

Spying is one of the oldest jobs in the world. Powerful people always want to know what other powerful people are up to. Until the late 20th century, the way people spied on each other stayed pretty much the same. Secret codes, hidden messages, undercover surveillance, and old-fashioned tricks, such as disguises, were the tools of all the world's spies. In 2001, though, it was clear that other techniques of spying were needed as well.

The 9/11 attacks broke open the secret world of U.S. spies in the CIA and other government agencies. The CIA, FBI, and other U.S. intelligence agencies were riddled with problems.

A SPY'S LIFE MYTHS: Q & A

Q: Will I have to work out every day?

A: Not unless you want to. Secret agents don't have superhuman strength. But they are intelligent and able to make thoughtful decisions. Think Black Widow, not the Hulk.

Officials were slow to adopt new technologies and ideas. This Cold War mind-set wasn't going to work anymore.

Although many different international spies heard intel about 9/11, the information was fragmented and incomplete. Reports went to different agencies, just as in the United States. After the attacks on 9/11, it was easy to look back and see how many warnings had come in. But at the time no one knew to connect the dots, or even how many dots there were.

Today, world threats no longer come from single, big countries or gory world wars. Spies from around the world battle shadowy, unseen enemies who work in small and relatively independent groups spread out over many different countries. These terrorists use their spy craft globally, taking advantage of the Internet to infiltrate their enemies. Today, one person with a laptop can bring down a country.

U.S. intelligence agencies learned their lessons from 9/11, and international spy groups also paid attention. Within the U.S. organizations, agents share more intel. A U.S. government organization, the National Counterterrorism Center (NCC), was created in 2003 just so the different agencies could communicate. The NCC is made up of high-level agents from many different agencies. Their goal is to share intelligence within the United States, and with agencies around the world whether they're U.S. agents working for the CIA, British agents with the Secret

Intelligence Service (MI6), or French agents with the General Directorate for External Security (DGSE), to try to ensure no one is caught by surprise by a big attack again.

WHEN IS A SPY NOT "A SPY"?

Not all clandestine operatives are called "spies," even though they're all working deep within the spy world. Say you're working for the CIA in a foreign country. You don't look or sound anything like the local people, but you need to get information without raising suspicion. How do you do it? Find someone to do the spying for you. You, the CIA operative who recruits new local spies, are not a spy. You're an officer (or handler, or core collector). Who are the spies? The locals you recruit to work for you. They are called agents (or assets, or spies) and they're the ones who will do all the spying. The handler trains the new agent, and then sends him or her off to gather intel. People often use "spy" and

Anna Chapman was part of an extensive undercover group of Russian spies living in the United States.

CHAPTER 18

FAKE CITIZENS, FAKE LIVES: HIDING IN PLAIN SIGHT

The grainy FBI surveillance video began by showing an empty staircase. Then a man appeared, carrying shopping bags. He started to climb. A second man appeared at the top of the staircase, going down. He also carried a handful of bags. So far, nothing unusual: just two strangers minding their own business after a day of shopping. Then the video got interesting. As the two figures passed on the staircase, they quickly switched bags without stopping. A few seconds later, they disappeared.

Those men weren't innocent shoppers. They were Russian agents, part of a sleeper cell of spies in the United States. Their mission? To go undercover, living as Americans, to send as much secret information back to Russia as they could. That bag-switching move, called a brush-pass, is something spies use all the time to exchange information.

Eleven Russian spies had come to the United States undercover to gather information. They had signed on for the mission knowing that it would go on for years. It's not clear exactly when they arrived in the United States but some had already begun their mission as far back as 2001, possibly even earlier than that.

They were instructed to become part of American society, so no one would ever suspect they were highly trained, expert agents. Their long-term mission was to infiltrate political circles and make contacts with people in the U.S. government. They were to gather information on U.S. nuclear weapons, rumors and information on Congress, the White House, and U.S. foreign policy.

What they didn't know was that the FBI had been on to them from the beginning. For 10 years U.S. spies watched the Russians' every move. They set up dozens of video surveillance cameras and watched their calls and emails. On June 27, 2010, the FBI ended the Russian spies' mission by arresting 10 of the 11 spies (one spy, known as Christopher Metsos, escaped and is still at large). The spies' names and photos were splashed all over the Internet and in newspapers around the world. It was the biggest Russian spy roundup in the United States in more than 20 years.

NORMAL PEOPLE, SECRET LIVES

The first thing people noticed about these highly secretive, deeply dangerous spies was how normal they looked. Male and female agents worked as undercover husband and wife teams, and some of them had children together. They went to school, bought houses, and had everyday jobs. To everyone they met, they seemed like ordinary, even boring, American families.

Hidden in their normal-looking lives, they used a mix of old spy tricks and modern technology to gather information and pass it on. The "brush pass" was only one of the dozens of ways they passed information to their Russian handlers. They used invisible ink and secret codes to pass messages, and kept hidden codebooks. Each agent used complex passwords to identify each other. One coded phrase was, "Excuse me, but haven't we met in California last summer?" The password reply was "No, I think it was in the Hamptons." They gave their contacts code names like Cat and Parrot.

The arrest by the FBI of 10 spies living undercover in the United States made headline news.

DID YOU KNOW?

The FBI called their surveillance
operation on the Russian spies
"Operation Ghost Stories" because six
of the Russian spies had stolen the
identities of dead people.

One of their favorite ways to pass information was by sitting in outdoor coffee shops or bookstores with their laptops. Who would suspect someone sipping coffee and surfing the Internet? Their Russian contacts would drive by slowly. The spies then beamed information from their computers to the contacts' electronic devices. Sometimes they hid encrypted information in photos and then posted the photos online.

WHAT MAKES A GOOD SPY?

When the FBI arrested the Russian spies in 2010, one stood out to the public. Anna Chapman was a young, attractive redhead who perfectly fit the "sexy spy" profile. She soon became a celebrity worldwide. Chapman used her fame to become a model, and eventually to host her own Russian TV show. But while the world was taken with her good looks, they glossed over the real story: Chapman, like her fellow Russian agents, was an intelligent, highly trained spy. She and the other spies were chosen for the U.S. mission because of their skills with the English language and the ease with which they could adapt to other cultures.

Chapman and her fellow Russian spies were the cream of the spy crop in Russia. What do spies like Anna Chapman, and other international agents, have that no one else has?

Spies are supersmart. Chapman has an IQ of 162—an IQ considered to be "genius"—and earned a master's degree in economics while in Russia. But "smart" doesn't always mean "college degree." Take "Shami" (not his real name). He is a British secret agent who never went to college. It was his street smarts that made him perfect for his spy job. He conducts secret surveillance on suspected terrorist cells for MI5, the British Security Service.

But the most important thing that makes a good spy is honesty and integrity. That may sound strange, since it's in the spy job description to lie and cheat—and they must do that all the time. But a spy also has to be trustworthy, someone a contact, or another spy, will respect enough to pass information to and even risk their lives for. Open, pleasant people who make friends easily

A SPY'S LIFE MYTHS: Q & A

Q: I'll never see my friends and family again, right?

A: Your job is a secret, but you'll still have a life. You might travel around the world, or you might work in a cubicle every day. Either way, you can have a family and friends.

DID YOU KNOW?

Most secret agents don't have the
power to arrest anyone. When it's
time to arrest the bad guy, an agent
has to call the police just like
everyone else.

make great spies. Anna Chapman and the other Russian agents were great at this. Their mission was to become "American," and they did it so well that when they were arrested, their American friends and neighbors were stunned. All the spies lived in normal suburban neighborhoods. Two of the Russians, Michael Zottoli (Mikhail Kutsik) and Patricia Mills (Natalia Pereverzeva) used to take walks through their Seattle neighborhood with their son. Another spy, Mikhail Semenko, posted online that he loved the New Jersey Devils hockey team. Cynthia Murphy (Lydia Guryev) loved gardening and planted hydrangeas in her yard while her two daughters rode their bikes. If this all sounds normal and boring, it's supposed to. The less threatening a spy is, the better chance he or she will have to gain someone's trust.

As well as infiltrating "normal" neighborhoods in the United States, the sleeper Russian agents relied on high-tech spying. Their Russian-made laptops were secretly loaded with a private wireless network that only communicated with the other spies' computers. They exchanged information and

Cynthia Murphy (Lydia Guryev) was a Russian undercover spy in the United States for many years.

kept records of their spy activities on the laptops. The FBI needed those laptops, and they found a way to get them. An undercover agent posed as a Russian-speaking fellow spy and offered to fix one laptop that wasn't working properly. The Russian agent fell for his story and handed over the laptop. The whole spy ring was arrested a few weeks later.

Although the Russian spy ring never got their hands on any real, secret intelligence, they came dangerously close. Eventually, all the Russians were exchanged for several U.S. spies that the Russian government had caught.

A SPY'S LIFE MYTHS: Q & A

Q: Do I have to speak several foreign languages?

A: If you can, all the better. If not, it's not a problem. If you get a mission in which you do need to know another language, you'll learn it.

Spying in the digital age adds a new dimension to gathering information.

CHAPTER 19

World Threat: Cyber Spying

Spies know each other. Or maybe they don't. They work together in groups. Or they work alone. They sit in dark rooms, bent over glowing computer screens. Or they hang out in brightly lit cafés. No one knows. Cyber spy groups are some of the biggest threats to world security. The scary part is that no one knows who they are, where they live, or how they work.

One international spy ring, purported to be the biggest in the world, has an innocent-sounding name: Emissary Panda. But what they do is anything but cute and cuddly. This shadowy group of cyber spies has been stealing information from military and political organizations around the world. They've taken emails, documents, data, and records that could destroy organizations. Their hacking mission is called Iron Tiger. No one knows who the members of Emissary Panda are, but they are based in China.

Emissary Panda, also known as Threat Group 3390, started by attacking companies in Asia. By 2013, they got bolder, hacking into the computer systems of high-tech companies in Europe and the United States. They also targeted embassies and organizations located in Russia, Iraq, Italy, Zambia, Afghanistan, and other countries in Africa, Europe, and the Middle East. They knew exactly what they were doing, targeting specific companies that specialized in military, intelligence, nuclear engineering, and communications. They chose their victims carefully and spent years getting into systems that held the most secret information.

Alarmingly, Emissary Panda changed their strategy around 2014. Before that, they would take everything they could find. Suddenly the spies slowed down, taking as long as two weeks to explore a hacked system and make long lists of the data they found. Then they'd carefully choose very specific files to steal.

THE FIRST CYBER SPY

In 1986, a German hacker named Markus Hess was recruited by the KGB, the Russian secret police. Hess' top-secret mission: to hack into world military and government systems and steal secrets. Hess managed to break into 30 computer systems in West Germany, Japan, and the United States and then sell the information to the KGB. He was caught and found guilty of computer espionage—the first ever convicted cyber spy.

For instance, a system might have thousands of secret files, but Emissary Panda would only steal two or three. That means the group is probably not stealing to make money. No one knows what the hacking group is doing with the information, but it's possible that they're working for someone, or some group, who tells them what to take.

Emissary Panda isn't the only world cyber spy group hacking its way through global computer systems. A Russian-speaking spy group launched a huge cyber attack around 2007. U.S. counterspies dubbed it "Red October," after a 1990 U.S. film called *The Hunt for Red October*. These Red October spies had very specific goals in mind: stealing information from diplomatic agencies around the world. They mostly targeted countries in Eastern Europe and Asia, but evidence of their spying has turned up in Western European and U.S. systems, too. Their victims are government agencies, embassies, consulates, and scientific research groups that have government and military secrets.

WORLD SPY CYBER TRICKS

Emissary Panda and Red October spies might have been from different countries but they used the same cyber spy tricks to steal secrets. The easiest was a trick called "spear phishing" to get passwords and other information used to break into computer systems. First they targeted specific people who had access to secrets and classified intelligence. The spies looked them up on social media to find out things such as the restaurants they went to, where they shopped, and who their friends were.

Then the real spying started. Emissary Panda sent fake emails to their targets. The emails looked like they were from friends, or from places that person had visited. Buried inside those emails was spyware that was automatically downloaded into the target's computer. The spyware let the spies break into that computer and get into the entire system. From there, they stole more classified information, passwords, and codes, and used those to break into other systems.

Both sets of international spies knew that most of the stolen intelligence would not be well protected. Even the best security programs can have bugs and holes that good hackers can find. Although the spies were experienced hackers, it didn't take much effort to get what they wanted.

The Iron Tiger hack wasn't a total surprise to the CIA and other U.S. spies. The Red October attack didn't come as a big surprise to European leaders, either. They'd been working to protect government computers from this kind of global cyber attack for years. After 9/11, the CIA and other world agencies became even more convinced that the next attacks would come from the Internet. Terrorist groups, they thought, would use the Internet to break into organizations and do physical damage to industry, communications, or transportation systems around the world. Cyber agents were trained to watch for these threats.

So far, there has been only one cyber terrorism attack like that anywhere in the world. In 2010, an Iranian nuclear power plant was attacked by Stuxnet, a virus that broke down machinery and computer systems. However, cyber spies are generally more interested in information, secrets, and classified documents. Cyber espionage remains the big threat of the 21st century.

EDWARD SNOWDEN: THE ULTIMATE CYBER SPY

On May 20, 2013, a quiet man boarded a plane traveling from the United States to Hong Kong. A few days later, in Hong Kong, he met with journalists from the United Kingdom. He told them his name was Edward Snowden, and he used to work with the U.S. National Security Agency (NSA). As part of his computer job at the NSA, he saw top-secret files. He stole them—millions of them—and then fled the country.

Why did he steal the files? The files revealed that the NSA was spying on ordinary Americans. The more Snowden saw how much the United States was spying on its own citizens, the angrier he got. He finally decided to do something about it by revealing those secrets to the world. The stolen files revealed how large U.S. companies such as Microsoft and Verizon gave the

Edward Snowden stole millions of cyber documents from the NSA.

NSA vast amounts of data and information on their customers.

Snowden revealed even more disturbing information about NSA spying. The NSA spied on computers that weren't connected to the Internet. The NSA paid software companies millions of dollars to create security programs with a "back door," allowing the NSA to spy on any company that used them. The NSA even tapped the phone calls of world leaders.

Journalists published Snowden's story and the world exploded at the news. The U.S. government charged Snowden with "theft of government property" and other charges under the Espionage Act. Not long after the leaks went public, Snowden disappeared from Hong Kong.

Eventually, Snowden arrived in Russia, where he lives today. Snowden continues to release these documents, and he says he has millions more.

DID YOU KNOW?

A movie called *Snowden* was released
in 2016 about Edward Snowden's cyber
spying. An NSA retired deputy director
said the movie exaggerated many things
and mischaracterized the NSA.

SPIES ON THE HUNT

One of the best ways cyber agents collect information is through cyber cafés. A cyber café is a shop, anywhere in the world, filled with computers that anyone can use for a small fee. Cyber cafés are often tucked away on side streets of cities such as London, Paris, Bangkok, Beijing, Cairo, and others. Many of them are near foreign embassies, religious buildings, international businesses, and other places a terrorist might frequent.

Most people who use cyber cafés think they are safe and anonymous. The reality is that some international cyber cafés were built by U.S. and British cyber agents. They watched what

OLD-SCHOOL SPYING MEETS COMPUTER TECH

Most world cyber agents spy on terrorist groups using both old-school spying skills and 21st century computer technology. The old fashioned, but very useful "dead drop" trick is perfect for cyber spies. One spy goes to a cyber café, library, or other public spot with Internet and downloads information into a public computer. The second spy comes along later and uploads that information. Sometimes the secret info is embedded in innocent looking emails, or in hidden codes within documents or photos.

websites people visited, monitored their browser history, recorded passwords and logins, and even planted spyware. It was a great way to look for terrorist activity.

U.S. agents closed most of their fake cyber cafés but they still use some to communicate with other foreign agents. In 2013, American spy Ryan Fogle was caught by Russian agents. They accused him of trying to recruit a Russian counter-agent to pass secrets to the U.S. government. The proof? A letter from him to his Russian counter-agent that explained how to make contact at a cyber café.

Agencies around the world will sometimes advertise for good
recruits for clandestine work.

CHAPTER 20

CLANDESTINE RECRUITING: LOOKING FOR A FEW GOOD SPIES

Spy Camp. It sounded like the coolest summer camp ever to a specially select group of Washington, D.C., high school students. In the summer of 2005, the students spent a week at Spy Camp. Instead of swimming and canoeing, the group went behind the scenes at CIA headquarters in Langley, Virginia. Rather than doing arts and crafts, they toured the Spy Museum and joined in scavenger hunts where teams had to practice code breaking and other spy skills.

The teens didn't know it, but the camp wasn't just for fun. It was created by Trinity University in Washington D.C., and a U.S. spy agency called the Office of National Intelligence (ONI). Its purpose is to find and recruit new spies. Spy Camp was part of a bigger program: the Intelligence Community Centers for Academic Excellence.

Today there are more than 20 spy camps (now called Summer Intelligence Seminars) and other secret agent camps

Students in Spy Camp work together to solve different problems.

on college campuses around the United States every summer. Some have high school programs, where kids learn spy tricks, such as using GPS to locate hidden (not real) weapons of mass destruction around a city.

The ONI didn't expect anyone to drop out of school and become a spy. But finding future secret agents is serious business for spy agencies all over the world, not just in the United States.

THE SECRET TO FINDING SECRET AGENTS

Most of the time, finding good spies is like finding good people to work in any job. The secret is that looking for them isn't a secret at all.

The big spy agencies like the CIA and Britain's MI6 go all out to find recruits. In 2011, Britain's top code-cracking and spy organization, Government Communications Headquarters (GCHQ), took recruitment online. They created a website called "Can You Crack It" with a mysterious cryptographic puzzle. The site challenged anyone to solve it. The lucky few who cracked the code were rewarded with a secret congratulatory message and the link to another website where the person could apply for a job as a code-cracking spy with GCHQ.

Spy groups don't just use camps and codes to find new agents. World espionage organizations have websites and YouTube commercials showing how awesome being a spy can be. In 2015, the British spy agency MI6 launched a huge recruitment campaign linked to the release of the James Bond movie *Spectre*. The campaign asked for recruits who wanted to "explore the human side of global intelligence."

In 2016, Britain's Ministry of Defence put an ad in the British Army's official magazine, *Soldier*. The advertisement showed a woman standing at a bus stop reading a newspaper. Next to it, a caption read: "This woman has vital information . . . Do you have the skills to find out what it is?"

A secret military group called the Defence Human Intelligence Unit (DHU) was behind the ad. They were looking for volunteers to fight ISIS and other terrorist groups. But the recruits wouldn't be shipped overseas. These secret agents would work on the streets of the United Kingdom. The DHU's agents would go undercover all over Britain, dressed in plainclothes, and no one would know who they were. Their only job would be to observe and record events as they happened on the street, in real time.

SPY SKILLS 101

Even if you are a master hacker or a code breaker, there are some basic requirements to being a spy in most countries. You have to be a citizen of the country you want to spy for. There's usually an age requirement, and some countries such as the United States would prefer agents with university degrees. Recruits usually have to pass a drug test, a credit check, and a criminal background check. They might have to take a lie-detector test. All of that is just the first step.

Recruits who meet those requirements move on to the next step. Spies don't have to speak different languages, but they do have to be skilled at learning them. Additionally, good spies have good social skills and can make friends easily.

The next part is trickier. No matter what country you're spying for, only recruits who can handle high stress and daily pressure will make it through. Can you go without sleep for long periods of time? How do you handle discomfort? What will you do when faced with instant danger? If you can think on your feet and stay cool-headed in a crisis, you might be spy material.

Finally, many spies must work undercover, so recruits have to be willing to lie to everyone they know, including friends, family, and coworkers (if they have a "cover" job). It may sound easy, but this part is sometimes the hardest to do. If you're good at hiding the truth, then you could be a spy.

GLOBAL SPY SCHOOLS THAT DON'T EXIST

The Farm. Fort Monckton. The University. These boring-sounding facilities hide a huge secret: each one of them is a secret spy school somewhere in the world. New recruits are sent to these schools to learn the top-secret tricks to being a world-class agent.

The Farm, near Williamsburg, Virginia, is the CIA training camp where U.S. recruits learn the business of spying. The camp is surrounded by a chain-link fence and no one is allowed in or out without permission. Fort Monckton, near Gosport, Hampshire, is the British ground zero for spy training. It's a real stone fort, and recruits must enter through an ancient drawbridge. The University, in Germany, is a sprawling facility in a secret location that few outside the German secret service know about.

Secret spy schools might be spread across the globe, but their spies-in-training have a lot in common. They all have to take classes with cool-sounding names like "Picks and Locks," "Code Breaking," and "Breaking and Entering." Recruits learn how to bug phones, read maps, exchange packages, open sealed envelopes, and interrogate suspects. At The University, German recruits focus on legal questions such as how to deal with a kidnapping in a foreign country. They study history, religion, politics, and geography. They learn how to recognize a liar. And that's just the classroom work.

On the outdoor training grounds at Fort Monckton and The Farm, British and U.S. recruits learn how to assemble and shoot different weapons, learn about different kinds of foreign weapons, and practice handling explosives. They train to shoot in every kind of weather condition and climate, from desert to blizzard. At the Farm, they spend hours training in hand-to-hand combat and martial arts skills such as krav maga and jiu jitsu.

Modern spies usually don't find themselves in dramatic car chases like in the movies, but in case they do, they learn how to drive and survive. Recruits at The Farm and The University learn how to use their car as a weapon or as protection from terrorists. At The Farm, U.S. recruits learn how to spin their own car and how to drive from the passenger seat if their driver is shot dead. Escape training includes high-speed driving around corners without losing control of the car.

Once a recruit graduates from any of these spy schools, it's time to go out into the field. Each U.S. recruit is assigned a city where former undercover FBI agents try to discover them and blow their cover. Recruits who pass this final test are official secret agents.

SPIES FINDING SPIES

An officer's hardest job is finding recruits from other countries who are willing to pass secrets. Every officer needs to establish trusted contacts around the world. Recruiting spies for their personal spy network is job number one.

First, an officer identifies the kinds of information she wants. The officer can target an individual who might have that information, or she can find a "principal agent" to help.

A SPY'S LIFE MYTHS: Q & A

Q: Will I get a fast car?

A: Car chases aren't part of a spy's job description. But you will learn how to drive any type of car to escape danger—no "fast" cars needed.

VALERIE PLAME

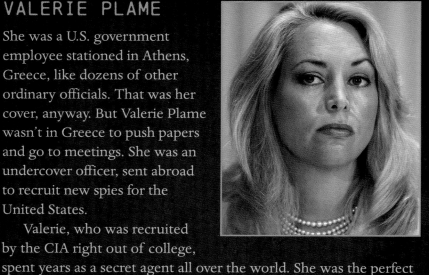

She was a U.S. government employee stationed in Athens, Greece, like dozens of other ordinary officials. That was her cover, anyway. But Valerie Plame wasn't in Greece to push papers and go to meetings. She was an undercover officer, sent abroad to recruit new spies for the United States.

Valerie, who was recruited by the CIA right out of college, spent years as a secret agent all over the world. She was the perfect spy: smart, capable, and not afraid of either danger or the loneliness that is part of a spy's life. By the mid-1990s she became one of the CIA's top NOCs (non-official cover agents). NOCs are the most secret of secret agents. They are the same as Russia's "illegals" or other countries' deep-cover spies. They don't have cover government jobs to keep their identities safe. Even more dangerous, the United States doesn't acknowledge them at all and gives them no protection. Valerie told everyone she was a businesswoman with an international company, but she still recruited spies for the United States.

It all went bad in the summer of 2003. The Bush administration claimed Iraq's leader, Saddam Hussein, had weapons of mass destruction. U.S. spies, however, couldn't find evidence of any weapons. In July, Valerie's husband, former ambassador Joe Wilson, wrote a newspaper article that accused the administration of making up evidence to justify war. Someone in the Bush administration leaked to the press that Valerie was an undercover agent; according to Joe Wilson and many others, her name was leaked in retaliation for Wilson's article. Valerie's cover was blown and her days as a secret agent were over. She wrote a book, *Fair Game* (that later became a movie by the same name), about her experiences, and now lives a quiet life with Joe in Santa Fe, New Mexico, far from the spy world she once lived in.

The principal agent is someone who fits into the group or culture and speaks the same language. That person scouts around to find others in the group who might be interested in turning into a spy.

For German spies, getting sources is one of their top jobs. One German spy had a tough assignment: recruiting an asset and getting him to trust her. She only had an hour and a half to do it. In that time she managed to find out about his job, his hobbies, and even his daughter's college test scores. She gained his trust, and with it, a new recruit.

Another way spies get other spies on their side is through "walk-ins." These people ask to join up and steal secrets from their countries. They do this for a lot of reasons. Most of them want money for their secrets. Some are angry at their companies, or their government, and want to punish them.

Once these new spies are recruited, they learn how to secretly pass along the information they've been asked to steal. Often the spy will have a secret location or a safe house where they can meet their officer to get assignments and exchange information.

Those who work at the U.S. National Reconnaissance Office design and build spy satellites.

CHAPTER 21

SPYING IN THE 21ST CENTURY AND BEYOND

Today's enemies are not just big armies or scary governments with nuclear weapons. Terrorist groups are small, mobile, and anonymous. They can stay invisible until they attack, and then do tremendous damage. These groups can be anywhere, at any time. They don't play by any of the rules that most governments are used to.

Spies in the 21st century must be trained to meet these new threats. They don't want to go to war—their job is to do everything they can to avoid it. To do that, every country needs information to run their governments and to watch for enemies. Global spies must know how to get any kind of information, anywhere, at any time. Where is all this new information coming from? Modern spies put a new spin on all the old tricks spies have always used, including human contacts, high-tech spying, and good old-fashioned research to meet new 21st century threats.

HUMINT: PERSON-TO-PERSON SPYING

HUMINT, or human intelligence, forms the basis of spying. Human officers gather information on the ground by creating relationships and trust with sources and other spies. Today, many officials believe that HUMINT is more important than ever, both for the United States and the world spy community.

How does HUMINT work? An agent gets a tip from an informant or a friend—a human source. Sometimes that means interrogating a witness. Other HUMINT can come from espionage or other secret sources. Most countries have their own intelligence divisions that focus on HUMINT. In the United States, HUMINT gathering is the job of the CIA. In Britain, MI6 is responsible for HUMINT.

The United States has been behind in HUMINT compared to other countries, mainly because U.S. agents concentrated on using technology to spy during the Cold War. France, China, and Russia have strong, well-established HUMINT capabilities around the world.

SIGINT: SPY FROM THE SKY

Ever heard of spy satellites? They collect SIGINT, or Signals Intelligence, which is information sent electronically. Ships, planes, computers, and satellites gather SIGINT every day. The United States is ahead of everyone else in the world when it comes to SIGINT. There's even a special U.S. intelligence agency, the National Reconnaissance Office, that employs people to build and maintain U.S. spy satellites.

U.S. SIGINT gathering is so advanced because it started more than 60 years ago, during the space race in the late 1950s in the midst of the Cold War. In 1959, a series of rockets blasted off from Onizuka Air Force Station in California. The National Aeronautics and Space Administration (NASA) told the press it was a mission called Discoverer. The Discoverer rockets were designed to test engineering systems, launching systems, and other systems needed for space flight.

A SPY'S LIFE MYTHS: Q & A

Q: I can't wait to get all the spy gadgets. I do get gadgets, don't I?

A: Agents do use cool technology as well as old-school spyware, such as invisible ink and hollow pens. When you get an assignment, you get the gadgets that are needed to go with it. What kind of gadgets will you have? That's classified.

Rockets take satellites to space.

The top-secret information NASA didn't share with the world was that Discoverer was a code name for a project even more secret. The project was so undercover that it had a second code name: Corona. The Corona program was a secret spy mission to send cameras into space using Corona satellites. The Corona was the United States' first spy satellite. It's biggest mission: to spy on the Soviet Union.

Deep inside those Discoverer rockets were their true payload: Corona spy satellites equipped with two 5-foot-long (1.5-m-long) cameras. The cameras were so high-tech that they could take clear black-and-white, 3-foot (1-m) close-ups of anything on Earth.

Since then, the United States and other countries have launched dozens of spy satellites into orbit. But it's not just about photos any more. In today's high-tech world, SIGINT includes the kind of information a spy can gather electronically. A basic spy trick all intelligence agencies use involves tapping phone lines and secretly listening in on conversations. SIGINT spy satellites do that on a global scale.

These satellites detect and monitor every kind of broadcast communication: radio, television, telephone, electronic systems,

SOLVING THE MYSTERY OF MALAYSIA FLIGHT 17 WITH MASINT

On July 17, 2014, a Malaysia Airlines commercial flight was downed over Ukraine, killing 283 passengers and 15 crew members. Immediately, world spy agencies suspected that the plane was shot down by a missile. But how could they prove it? With MASINT (spying on weapons), spy satellites can detect a missile launch anywhere in the world, tracking it by its heat signature. U.S. spies analyzed this data from satellites to determine that the missile was a Soviet-era Buk missile, launched either from Russia or Ukraine. Both governments admit they use Buk missiles, but both also denied they shot down the plane. No definitive answer has been found at this time.

and even other satellites. They can also follow electronic transmissions from weapons tests or enemy radar systems. They can pinpoint locations where the broadcasts or messages come from, and their computer systems can decrypt coded messages. The only downside to these powerful spy satellites is that they can't pick up messages sent on landlines such as fiber-optic underground or undersea cables.

France, Italy, and Germany all have a few spy satellites in orbit and some spy networks on land and sea in Europe and around the world. But these countries' spies are best in HUMINT. That puts agents in a good position to trade secrets, exchanging intel gathered through SIGINT in return for information gathered from HUMINT sources.

MASINT: SPYING ON WEAPONS

How can you spy on a weapon? One word: technology. High-tech weapons send information and data through their computer systems. Specially trained spies can hack into the weapons' computer systems, and use Measurement and Signature Intelligence (MASINT) to steal or monitor useful information, such as where the weapons are, how they work, and what they target. Then the agents analyze the data to get the most information. For instance, MASINT can be used to find chemical weapons, or to identify chemical parts of unknown weapons.

MASINT comes in many different ways. For instance, acoustic intel is information based on sound. Different weapons or systems make different sounds, clueing a spy in on which weapon is making that noise without seeing the weapon itself. Seismic intel can be ground-shaking—literally. Agents monitor how much the ground shakes when a weapons target rolls past to determine its size and strength.

OSINT: INTEL IN PLAIN SIGHT

Facebook, Twitter, Tumblr, Snapchat, television, radio, magazine articles, reports, speeches, newspapers, and public records are everywhere. The best spies know how to get information from these public, or open, sources, called Open Source Intel (OSINT). Most agents use a combination of OSINT and other intelligence gathering to get as much information as possible. Government spy organizations in the United States, Britain, Australia, Israel, China, and Russia all have OSINT divisions. But it's not just spies who use OSINT. Because terrorists can strike anywhere, in any city in the world, law-enforcement agencies such as Interpol (Europe), Scotland Yard (Britain), the Royal Canadian Mounted Police, and police departments in New York and Chicago (United States) have created OSINT squads.

Sometimes the Internet makes it easy for anyone, not just agents, to spy on the world. Google Earth was a big game-changer in the global world of OSINT spying. Now anyone can look in on any country on Earth, and see whether it is gathering an army or building weapons. The best OSINT targets are organizations in countries that have good Internet and telecommunications. In an era when terrorist groups have their own magazines and YouTube channels, it's not hard to find and monitor world threats with OSINT.

The problem is that there is so much information it can be hard for an intelligence analyst to figure out what's most important. They spend hours, or days, surfing the Internet, looking for bits of intel that might help them with a mission. Most OSINT spies are good at foreign languages, so they can read websites and intel from many countries.

MODERN SPY GADGETS

Today's spies use the latest gear in their classified missions. A lot of their technology involves 21st century versions of the best spy tricks agents have used for years.

Back in the old-school spy days, "remote monitoring," or listening in on someone's conversations, meant planting electronic "bugs" in homes or on telephones. Back then that meant a spy had to break into a home or business, plant a bug in a hidden location, and hope no one found it. Today's global spies don't have to resort to breaking and entering (although they learn how to do so in spy school.) Dozens of everyday objects come already equipped with bugs. Does an agent need to put a secret surveillance camera in someone's home? Just pose as an electrician and install electrical outlets with their own hidden cameras. Even better is a fake smoke alarm that is really a video camera with a motion detector and night vision. Clocks, pens, buttons, neckties, and even air fresheners come with their own cameras and monitoring devices.

Sometimes spies need to break into someone's computer. The days when a cyber spy spent days, or weeks, trying to figure out passwords is long gone. Today's spies plant a keylogger on the computer. This handy spy gadget records every keystroke that anyone types, and keeps track of passwords and email. Sometimes an agent can load a keylogger program onto a computer. Keylogger software can be secretly installed from a website the spy has infected with the program. Other keyloggers are small devices that plug into the computer and send the information remotely.

Cyber spy groups like Emissary Panda and Red October used keyloggers to steal secrets. CIA and MI6 agents used them in fake cyber cafés to monitor users' emails and conversations.

Following a target has always been a basic spy job. Movies and TV shows are full of spies planting electronic tracking devices on cars. Modern spies now have high-tech GPS devices that can track everything from the route, speed, direction, and even altitude of a vehicle. Not only that, but all this information can be downloaded into the spy's computer and saved.

Ordinary writing pens have often been turned into some of the best spy gadgets. They can hold cameras, microphones, and recording devices. Today, secret spy pens can be used as document scanners, with the ability to quickly and clearly copy secret messages and other classified documents.

Most people carry loose change, and what better way to hide messages and secret information than in a coin? Hollow coins have been a spy's go-to gadget since the Cold War, and they're still as useful today as they were back then. Years ago spies used hollow coins to hide microfilm or suicide poison. Today's spies are more likely to hide a computer SD card. The biggest danger with these secret coins? Forgetting they're not real coins and spending them.

OLD-SCHOOL SPYING MAKING A COMEBACK

The more that spies rely on computers and other high-tech devices, the more they find out how unreliable they can be. The more that countries around the world rely on electronics and computers, the easier it becomes for anyone with a laptop to break into classified and secret files. Modern spies in the United States and Britain are packing away their computers and high-tech devices and returning to plain old HUMINT. What that means is spies are going back to using face-to-face meetings and hands-on surveillance. They're making connections in the real world with

DID YOU KNOW?

In 2018, a new super-spy reconnaissance satellite will blast into space, code-named NROL-71. It's so top secret and classified that very few people know what kind of spy tech this new satellite has.

real people to gather the intelligence they need.

Computer systems have become so easy to hack that most enemies and terrorist groups have taken vital information offline for good. Instead, they're communicating with old-fashioned codes, cyphers, secret messages, short-wave radio transmissions, and real-world dead drops. Not only are these spy tricks effective, they're also free. Terrorist networks that don't have a lot of money for high-tech computers or other gear use the old-school spy techniques. The best 21st century spies will be experts at mixing old-world tricks with modern tech to catch the bad guys.

Spy tools can be hidden in everyday objects.

TIMELINE

June 28, 1914

Black Hand spy Gavrilo Princip assassinates Archduke Franz
Ferdinand of Austria-Hungary

July 28, 1914

Backed by Germany, Austria-Hungary declares war on Serbia
World War I begins

August 1, 1914

Germany declares war on Russia

August 3, 1914

Germany declares war on France

August 4, 1914

Germany declares war on Belgium
Britain declares war on Germany
The United States declares its neutrality

August 10, 1914

France declares war on Austria-Hungary

August 12, 1914

Britain declares war on Austria-Hungary

August 23, 1914

Germany invades France
Austria-Hungary invades Russian Poland
Japan declares war on Germany

August 27, 1914

Austria-Hungary declares war on Belgium

November 7, 1916

Woodrow Wilson is re-elected president of the United States with
the slogan, "He Kept Us Out of War"

January 17, 1917

Room 40 spies crack the Zimmerman telegram

April 6, 1917
The United States declares war on Germany, entering World War I

November 7, 1917
Vladimir Lenin and the Bolsheviks take over Russia, winning the
Russian Revolution

August 30, 1918
Fanya Kaplan tries to assassinate Vladimir Lenin

November 11, 1918
World War I ends

May 26, 1938
House Un-American Activities Committee is created

September 1, 1939
Hitler invades Poland, sparking World War II

September 3, 1939
Britain, France, Australia, and New Zealand declare war on
Germany

May 10, 1940
Germany invades the Netherlands

December 7, 1941
Japanese bomb Pearl Harbor

December 8, 1941
Japanese bomb U.S. military targets in the Philippines
United States and Britain declare war on Japan

December 11, 1941
Germany declares war on the United States
United States declares war on Germany

Summer, 1944
Richard and Filipino Resistance storm Mantinlupa Prison

August 25, 1944
Allies liberate Paris

April 30, 1945
Hitler commits suicide

May 8, 1945
Allies declare victory in Europe (VE Day)

August 1945
Korea is divided into North Korea and South Korea

August 6 & 9, 1945
United States drops atomic bombs on Hiroshima and Nagasaki, Japan

September 2, 1945
Allies declare victory in Japan (VJ Day), ending World War II

May 23, 1949
Germany is officially divided into West Germany (Federal Republic of Germany) and East Germany (German Democratic Republic)

June 25, 1950
North Korea invades South Korea, beginning the Korean War

July 27, 1953
The Korean War ends. North Korea and South Korea remain divided.

November 1, 1955
Vietnam is divided into North and South Vietnam. The Vietnam War begins.

1959
The first spy satellites, code-named Corona, are launched

May 1960
Soviet Premier Nikita Khrushchev promises Cuba he will defend it with Soviet missiles

August 13, 1961
Construction begins on the Berlin Wall dividing the German city of Berlin into East Berlin and West Berlin

October 22-28, 1962
The Cuban Missile Crisis

March 1965
First U.S. combat troops sent to Vietnam

April 30, 1975
The Vietnam War ends with Saigon falling to the North Vietnamese

November 9, 1989
The Berlin Wall falls

September 11, 2001
Terrorists hijack airplanes and fly them into both towers of the World Trade Center in New York, the Pentagon in Washington, D.C., and crashing in a field in Pennsylvania, killing almost 3,000 people

October 26, 2001
President George W. Bush signs the USA PATRIOT Act, which gives U.S. spy agencies greater power to gather intelligence

2010
Eleven Russian spies are arrested by the FBI and deported

2013
American spy Ryan Fogle is arrested in Russia.
Emissary Panda hackers break into classified government computer systems throughout the United States.
Edward Snowden leaks secret classified information to the world

October 2015
The CIA creates a new cyber crime division, the Directorate of Digital Innovation

GLOSSARY

alias—a different name for someone

assassinate—to murder someone who is well known

Bolshevik—Russian political party that took power in 1917, in favor of the working class seizing power

civilian—a person who is not part of the military

clandestine—secret

consecutive—in a row

conspirators—people who plan to commit something, usually harmful or illegal, together

consulate—a place where foreign officials conduct business

coroner—a medical professional who finds out how someone has died

counterintelligence—ways to stop an enemy from learning secrets

cyanide—salt of hydrocyanic acid, a fatal poison

decipher—to uncover or find the meaning

deliberations—conversations or thoughts to come to a decision

detonate—to go off or explode

dignitary—someone with a high rank or a high position

diplomatic pouch—a container sent to an embassy that isn't subject to inspection

dissenters—people who disagree, often publicly, with a position, person, or set of beliefs

dysentery—a disease that causes diarrhea and blood loss

Eastern Bloc—a group of countries under Soviet rule until the collapse of Soviet communism. Countries included the USSR, Poland, Albania, Ukraine, East Germany, Czechoslovakia, Hungary, Romania, Bulgaria, and Yugoslavia

encrypt—to encode a message

espionage—spying using human operatives

fascism—a government system of rule by a dictator, in which people are not permitted to challenge the country's authority

Gestapo—the German secret police from 1933 to 1945

handler—an intelligence officer who recruits a spy, and then trains and works with him or her

in absentia—in the absence of the person involved

infiltrate—to move into an area or group slowly and secretly

intercept—to stop something or someone before the destination is reached

intern—to confine or imprison, most often during a war

Japanese national—someone born in and a citizen of Japan

lenient—not being strict; providing a lot of freedom

martial law—when the military of a country suspends regular laws and takes over

martyr—a person who dies for a belief or cause

microfilm and microdots—very small photos

Morse code—a system of communication that uses sounds or lights in patterns of short or long bursts to convey information

nationalist—a person loyal to their country, often believing their country is better than others

naturalized—having become a citizen of a country, in which one was not born

operative—a secret agent or spy

propaganda—materials, often misleading or exaggerated, designed to persuade people to join a certain cause or movement

purported—it is said or believed, but might not be true

Resistance—the people of an invaded nation who work together to drive out the invaders, often in secret

SD card—a secure digital card that stores information

surveillance—keeping watch on a person or location

transmitter—a device for sending broadcasts

treachery—betraying a friend or country with harmful acts or words

tuberculosis—disease that affects the lungs and causes fever, cough, and difficulty breathing

underground—secret and done without government approval

visa—a stamp on a passport that allows the owner to travel into a country for a time

INDEX

The author and publisher are grateful to the following for permission to reproduce
copyright material:

Alamy: Chronicle, 30, 158, INTERFOTO, 76, SPUTNIK, 162, Sueddeutsche Zeitung Photo, 118;
AP Photo: 88, Charles Dharapak, 166; Courtesy of the Federal Bureau of Investigations: 95; Flickr:
Internet Archive Book Images, 43; Getty Images: 198, ALEXANDER NEMENOV, 190, Apic, 68,
Archive Photos, 124, Bettmann, 56, 101, 132, 154, BRENDAN SMIALOWSKI/AFP, 145, Bride
Lane Library/Popperfoto, 83, Central Press, 126, Chip Somodevilla, 218, Daniel Berehulak, 210,
EMMANUEL DUNAND/AFP, 193, Greg Mathieson/Mai/Mai/The LIFE Images Collection, 220,
Hulton Archive, 19, 36, Imagno, 111, IWM, 87, Keystone-France/Gamma-Keystone, 168, Mansell/
Time Life Pictures, 105, Michael Probst, 232, New York Daily News Archive, 147, Photo by Cedric
H. Rudisill/USAF/DOD, 186, Popperfoto, 44, 71, Time Life Pictures/The LIFE Picture Collection,
129, Universal Images Group, 183; The Image Works: Roger-Viollet, 48; Library of Congress: 14, 28,
94, 97; Newscom: akg-images, 17, 136 (all), Collection Jaime Abecasis imageBROKER, 55, Crown/
Mirrorpix, 148, Everett Collection, 25, 107, 139, 164, Gene Blevins/Polaris, 224, GUARDIAN/
GLENN GREENWALD/LAURA POITRAS, 206, HEINRICH HOFFMANN/EPA, 116, HUGH
VAN ES UPI Photo Service, 174, Keystone Pictures USA/ZUMA PRESS, 156, KRT, 98, Laura
Cavanaugh UPI Photo Service, 180, Marcio Machado/ZUMA Press, 12, picture-alliance/dpa,
108, UPPA/Photoshot, 142, World History Archive, 35, 46; Rex: Shutterstock/Len Cassingham/
Daily Mail, 79; Shutterstock: acid2728k, 177 (numbers), BERNATSKAYA OXANA, 65 (fire), Black
Russian Studio, 121 (US Capitol), Kaissa, 177 (arrow), Monkey Business Images, 212, Nickolay
Khoroshkov, 9 (street light), pixelparticle, 177 (lens flare), scyther5, 200, Shaun Jeffers, 65 (London
skyline), STILLFX, 121 (flag), Tom Reichner, 9 (evergreens), Venera Salman, 121 (rain), vichie81, 9
(mountains), wawritto, 121 (hammer & sickle); Wikimedia: 20, 80, 84